Tibetan Mastiff Ultimate Care Guide
Includes: Tibetan Mastiff Training, Grooming, Lifespan, Puppies, Sizes, Socialization, Personality, Temperament, Rescue & Adoption, Shedding, Breeders, and More

Dr Margaret Shepperton

Copyright © 2023 by Dr Margaret Shepperton

This e-book is copyright © protected.
You are in violation of software copyright protection laws in relation to an illegal upload and link to our software product if you give away a copy of this ebook. If you do so, legal proceedings will commence under copyright infringement laws and loss of earnings.
No part of this ebook may be reproduced, stored in retrieval systems, or transmitted by any means, electronic, mechanical, photocopying, recorded or otherwise without written permission from the author or publisher.

Acknowledgements

With grateful thanks to the many Tibetan Mastiff lovers out there who own or would like to own this wonderful breed of dog. Without you this book could not have gone from being an idea to becoming a formal book. You are a true inspiration. Thank You.

There are times in life when you come across unique individuals who are full of love and selfless in their nature. Thank you to the many dog breeders who have provided insights into breeding and raising dogs over the years. Without your commitment, we would have no pedigree dogs today.

Table of Contents

Table of Contents 4
Chapter One: Introduction to the Tibetan Mastiff 14
Chapter Two: Understanding the Tibetan Mastiff 17
    What is a Tibetan Mastiff? ....
    The History of the Tibetan Mastiff ....
    Breed standard of the Tibetan Mastiff ....
    Differences in Tibetan Mastiffs ....
    General facts about the Tibetan Mastiff ....
        Do Tibetan Mastiffs shed? ....
        Are Tibetan Mastiffs hard to train? ....
        Are Tibetan Mastiffs good with children? ....
        Do Tibetan Mastiffs get along with other pets? ....
        The Tibetan Mastiff as a watchdog ....
        Do Tibetan Mastiffs do well in all climates? ....
        How much do Tibetan Mastiffs cost? ....
        Living arrangements for Tibetan Mastiffs ....
Chapter Three: The Personality of the Tibetan Mastiff 31
Chapter Four: Finding A Tibetan Mastiff 34
    Finding a breeder ....
    A breeder who will answer questions ....
    A breeder who is active with the breed club and kennel club ....
    A breeder who does things with her dogs ....
    A breeder who can give you backgrounds on her dogs ....
    A breeder who has a puppy plan and health clearances ....
    Clean facilities ....
    Healthy dogs ....
    Paperwork ....
    Puppies raised indoors ....
    Good references ....
    What the breeder expects of you ....
    Adopting an Older Tibetan Mastiff ....
    Choosing your Tibetan Mastiff ....

Chapter Five: Getting Ready For Your Puppy 48
   General Supplies..
      Feeding Bowls ....
      Collar ....
      Leash...
      Dog Grooming Items ....
      Crate..
      Toys...
      Cleaning Supplies ....
      Dog Bed ....
      Additional Supplies ....
      Puppy Training Pads ....
      Baby Gates..
      Stress Reducing Items...................................
      Vitamins..
   Puppy Proofing your Home...............................
      Put up any hazardous items ....
      Puppy's eye view...
      Put knick-knacks up high...............................
      Close off access to standing water.................
      Tie up those electrical cords and drapery cords...................
      Keep garbage out of reach or in a puppy proof container ....
      Block off stairs..
      Keep doors closed...
      Check the outdoors ....
      Look at your plants ....
      Toxic Plants..
Chapter Six: Bringing Your Tibetan Mastiff Puppy Home 64
   The Day of Pick Up...
   Introducing your Tibetan Mastiff to other family members ....
      Children ....
      Other Pets...
   Socialization and the First Few Weeks.............
Chapter Seven: Caring for your Tibetan Mastiff.................81
   Daily Care..
      Feeding ....
      Watering...

Tibetan Mastiff

    Grooming ....
    Vaccinations ....
    Training and Socializing ....
    Exercise ....
    Bathroom Breaks ....
    Quality Time ....
Exercise ....
Grooming ....
    Bathing ....
    Nail Clipping ....
    Brushing ....
    Ears ....
    Teeth ....
Training ....
    a. "Sit!" ....
    b. "Stay!" ....
    c. "Down" ....
    d. "Come" ....
    e. "Focus" ....
    f. "Drop It!" ....
    g. "Leave It!" ....
    h. Housetraining ....
Chapter Eight: Feeding your Tibetan Mastiff 114
    Types of Food ....
        Food Type Number One: Dry Food ....
        Food Type Number Two: Wet Food ....
        Food Type Number Three: Semi-moist Food ....
        Food Type Number Four: RAW/Homemade Food ....
    Feeding your Tibetan Mastiff ....
        When to Feed ....
        How much to Feed ....
        How to Feed ....
        Watering your Tibetan Mastiff ....
    Treats for your Tibetan Mastiff ....
    Foods to Avoid ....
Chapter Nine: Socializing and Training your Tibetan Mastiff ... 138
    Socializing your Tibetan Mastiff ....

Tibetan Mastiff

What is Socialization?
When Should I Socialize?
How do I socialize?
What Should I Socialize To?
Training your Tibetan Mastiff
Chapter Ten: Tibetan Mastiff Health 152
Signs of Illness
- Bad Breath
- Drooling
- Loss of Appetite
- Excessive Thirst
- Changes in Urination
- Skin Problems
- Lethargy
- Gum Problems
- Changes in Weight
- Stiffness of Limbs
- Respiratory Problems
- Runny Eyes or Nose
- Vomiting and Gagging
- Fluctuations in Temperature

Common Health Problems in the Breed
- a) Hypothyroidism
- b) entropion
- c) ectropion
- d) distichiasis
- e) demodex
- f) Addison's Disease
- g) Cushing's Disease
- h) epilepsy
- i) progressive retinal atrophy (PRA)
- j) hip or elbow dysplasia

First Aid for your Tibetan Mastiff
- a) First Aid Kit
- b) Dealing with an Emergency
- c) CPR

Chapter Eleven: Breeding your Tibetan Mastiff 191

Choosing dogs to breed ....
   Breeding your Tibetan Mastiff ....
      The Heat...
      Natural or Artificial?..
      When to Breed ....
      The Act of Breeding...
      Is She Pregnant ....
   Whelping your Pups ....
      Whelping Supplies...
      Before Labour ....
      First Stage Labour...
      Second Stage of Labour ....
      Third Stage of Labour ....
   Raising Pups ....
Chapter Twelve: Saying Goodbye To Your Tibetan Mastiff 227
   Vet care for older dogs..
   Saying goodbye ....
      Grief..
Chapter Thirteen: Common Terms..233
Chapter Fourteen: Resources 269
   Tibetan Mastiff Resources ....
   Tibetan Mastiff Breeders ....
Kennel Clubs 271
   Dog Owner Resources ....

Tibetan Mastiff   **7**

Chapter One: Introduction to the Tibetan Mastiff

The Tibetan Mastiff has been something of a well-kept secret for centuries. Yet they are one of the most ancient breeds of dogs we have today. In the United States, Tibetan Mastiffs ranked 132nd out of 177 breeds in registration numbers. In the UK, the Kennel Club reported 73 Tibetan Mastiffs registered in 2013, up from 37 dogs registered 10 years earlier. The breed nearly died out in the West following World War II.

On the other side of the world, Tibetan Mastiffs are enjoying a tremendous surge in popularity in China and other Pacific Rim countries. These dogs, native to Tibet and the Himalayas, are often sold by Tibetan Mastiff breeders for large sums in China. There are reports of buyers paying several million dollars for a Tibetan Mastiff. The dogs have become a status symbol, signifying wealth, success, and a certain national pride.

If you're interested in the breed and just starting to learn about them, they are magnificent dogs. A Tibetan Mastiff can stand up to 33 inches tall at the shoulder and weigh 160 pounds or more. They are "flock guarding dogs," meaning that they have worked for centuries to guard flocks of sheep and yak and other animals from predators such as wolves and leopards. Living in a cold, mountainous region, the dogs developed a long, dense double-coat. Their coat comes in a wide range of colors, though red Tibetan Mastiffs are very popular.

Before you get a Tibetan Mastiff, you should know that these dogs are not for everyone. Not only are they extremely large, meaning they need some room and they eat a lot, but they are not cuddly dogs. Tibetan Mastiffs are considered to be a "primitive" breed. Even though the breed is very old, they still retain many undomesticated characteristics. They tend to be highly independent and more aloof than most dog breeds. They think for themselves and they can be stubborn. They can be an excellent family dog but they do require training and socialization. No one wants to get into a disagreement with a 160-pound dog over who is going to sit on the sofa. So, training needs to begin when a Tibetan Mastiff is a young puppy.

If you are very particular about keeping your home tidy and neat, then a Tibetan Mastiff might be a challenge for you. Like other primitive breeds, they usually have one large moult or shed once per year, which is helpful in terms of picking up dog hair. However, some Tibetan Mastiffs drool and slobber if they have loose jowls. Their large, furry paws can also track in a lot of dirt and mud. If you have your heart set on this handsome breed, these issues just go with the territory.

If you have a Tibetan Mastiff you will probably always feel safe and protected at home. These dogs are not typical guard dogs but they are more than able to keep watch and defend their families. These dogs are very protective so if you bring friends and family home with you, you will need to show your dog that your visitors are welcome.

Make no mistake about Tibetan Mastiffs and their protective side – these dogs are protectors but they are not killers. These are not fighting dogs.

Ancient, primitive, independent in nature, aloof, and physically imposing – the Tibetan Mastiff is a unique dog. They require a special owner and have some special needs. In this book you'll learn more about these remarkable dogs and how to care for them, from finding a Tibetan Mastiff breeder with Tibetan Mastiff puppies for sale, what to ask a breeder, to raising your Tibetan

Mastiff puppy, and the training they need. We'll also discuss health issues in the breed, the food they need (it takes a lot of good food to keep a Tibetan Mastiff healthy and active), and general care. You'll also find resources for further information at the back of the book.

If you're seeking information about the Tibetan Mastiff, you've come to the right place, so let's continue.

Chapter Two: Understanding the Tibetan Mastiff

Before getting any dog, it's always important to learn all you can about them and their background. This is true whether you are getting a pedigree dog or a mixed breed. Many dogs are surrendered to shelters and rescues because the dog was not a good match for the owner's lifestyle or the dog's temperament was not a good match. In this chapter we'll look at the Tibetan Mastiff's background in depth to help you determine if this breed would be a good match for you.

What is a Tibetan Mastiff?

The Tibetan Mastiff is a large, impressive dog with a noble but solemn expression. The breed dates back several thousand years and comes from the Himalayas where they were flock guarding dogs. They have a huge double coat that comes in black, brown, blue/grey, with or without tan markings, and various shades of gold – some of which appear red. The dogs are usually very independent and quite intelligent.

The History of the Tibetan Mastiff

The Tibetan Mastiff dates back to at least 1100 BC when there are written accounts of the dogs in China. The breed comes from Tibet and the Himalayas where they have always been used as flock guardian dogs to protect flocks from wolves and big cats. The dogs would typically guard the flocks at night, making them nocturnal. They would sleep during the day. When the flocks were moved to higher pastures, the dogs would stay behind to guard the nomadic families and their tents. Not only did they guard flocks, but they guarded the women and children in the camps. These are loyal and trustworthy dogs.

One theory claims that a large Tibetan guardian dog is the ancestor of all Mollossus (Mastiff) breeds and working dogs, though this theory is not accepted by everyone. Ancestors of many Mastiff breeds were used as war dogs by the armies of Rome, Persia, Greece, Attila the Hun, and Genghis Khan, among others, but the Tibetan Mastiff stayed home to guard the flocks. The breed was isolated during these centuries and developed into the breed that exists today.

Pure Tibetan Mastiffs are hard to find in Tibet, Nepal, Bhutan and other Himalayan regions. However, the dogs are still bred by the nomads of the Chang-Tang plateau. These nomads and their dogs live at an average altitude of 16,000 feet. Some of the dogs are brought to the market that surrounds Jokhang Temple which is the holiest temple for Tibetan Buddhists. Here you can find these pure Tibetan Mastiffs for sale.

Before 1800, few Westerners were allowed into Tibet, so they knew very little about Tibetan dogs. Marco Polo mentioned that the dogs in Tibet were as large as donkeys. Jesuit missionaries in the 17th century wrote about huge, ferocious dogs: "Many of the Thibetan dogs are uncommon and extraordinary. They are black with rather long glossy hair, very big and sturdily built, and their bark is most alarming" I. Desideri, 1712.

The Tibetan Mastiff has been relatively rare in the West. In the 19th century King George IV owned a pair of them. In 1847 the Viceroy of India sent a "large dog from Tibet" to Queen Victoria. When the Kennel Club formed the first Stud Book in 1873, they officially listed a large dog from Tibet as a "Tibetan Mastiff" for the first time. There were enough Tibetan Mastiffs in England in 1906 for the breed to be exhibited at the Crystal Palace show. In

1931 the Tibetan Breeds Association was formed in England and the first official standard for the breed was accepted by the Kennel Club. This was also the standard used by the Federation Cynologique Internationale (FCI). However, the breed virtually died out in Britain during the war years. (This is true for a number of breeds.)

The breed has also been rare in the United States. Two Tibetan Mastiffs were sent to President Eisenhower from Tibet in the 1950s. Starting in 1969, a number of Tibetan Mastiffs were imported into the U.S. from India and Nepal. The American Tibetan Mastiff Association was formed in 1974.

The breed was only recognized by the American Kennel Club in 2006 and appeared at the Westminster Kennel Club show for the first time in 2008. The AKC does not recognize a breed for registration purposes until there are enough breeders and dogs in the United States to sustain the breed, even if a breed is very old. For most people in the United States, the Tibetan Mastiff is a "new" breed today, even though the breed is thousands of years old.

Breed standard of the Tibetan Mastiff

Breeders and fanciers dedicated to improving a breed create official breed standards to describe a breed's physical appearance. Although these standards can differ slightly from one country and one registry to another, they are usually very similar throughout the world. You can check the chapter on Resources at the end of the book to find kennel clubs around the world that register the Tibetan Mastiff. These clubs will have their official breed standards for the breed.

If you are looking for a Tibetan Mastiff for sale, you can use the breed standard as a way to evaluate the dog's strengths and weaknesses, especially if he is an adult dog. It's a little more difficult to evaluate Tibetan Mastiff puppies and guess how they will look when they are adults. If you are interested in a puppy as a show prospect or want a puppy who will be a stunner when he grows up, you should get some expert advice when you look at puppies. Take someone with you who is an expert in the breed and who can judge how Tibetan Mastiff puppies will look when they are adults.

Overall, the Tibetan Mastiff is a powerful, heavy, well-built dog. They have plenty of bone. (This is a dog person's way of saying they have thick bones – suggesting they are sturdy.) They have a noble, solemn expression. They are robust, majestic, and strong. Endurance is one of their great traits. Despite their heavy coat, they are able to work in all kinds of climate.

As a breed they are slow to mature. Females can take 2 or 3 years to mature; and males can take 4 years or more. Unlike many giant breeds, the Tibetan Mastiff has a long lifespan. They often live to be 12 to 14 years. Many giant breeds, such as the Great Dane and Irish Wolfhound – of comparable size with the Tibetan Mastiff – will not live to be 10 years old.

The Tibetan Mastiff's head is broad, heavy, and strong. You may see adult dogs have a wrinkle from above the eyes down to the corner of the mouth. The skull is slightly rounded. The nose is broad and dark. It will be darker in dark-coloured dogs. The muzzle is fairly broad and it should be squared on the end. The jaws should be strong and the teeth should meet in a scissors bite (the top teeth should fit snugly over the bottom teeth). The eyes should be medium in size and they can be any shade of brown, but the darker the better. They should be set well apart, be oval, and slant slightly. They should also fit tightly with no loose eyelid showing. The eyes should have an expression of dignity.

The dog's ears are also medium in size. They should be triangular in shape and hang down. The neck is strong and arched, with good muscling. The neck has a thick mane of hair that stands up, especially in the males. There is less mane in the females.

The body is strong with a straight back. The chest is deep and moderately broad. There should be room for good rib spring. (Rib spring is what it sounds like – where the ribs spring out along the body. This gives the body plenty of room for the lungs and heart to function properly.)

The dog's tail is medium in length. It is set high so it comes off level with the back. Tibetan Mastiffs carry their tail high, often curled loosely over their back. There is good feathering on the tail.

The legs are powerful and well-muscled. The paws are large, round, strong, and compact. There should be good feathering between the toes.

The Tibetan Mastiff's top layer of coat is fine but harsh to protect against the elements. The top coat is not too long but it is straight and stands off from the body. The undercoat is dense and woolly in cold weather but it becomes thinner in warm weather. Males have much more coat than females. The neck and shoulders have lots of coat which looks like a mane. The tail is bushy. The hind legs have lots of feathering.

The coat colours for the Tibetan Mastiff include rich black, with or without tan markings; blue, with or without tan markings; gold, ranging from rich fawn to deep red; and sable. The tan markings range from a rich chestnut to lighter shades. Some dogs have a white star on the chest and some dogs have white markings on their paws. Dogs who have tan markings have them over their eyes and on their legs and below their tails.

Size for adult Tibetan Mastiffs (height at the withers)

Dogs : 66 cm (26 inches) minimum
Bitches: 61 cm (24 inches) minimum

Many dogs will be larger than these minimum heights.

In terms of proportion, Tibetan Mastiffs are slightly longer than they are tall by a 10:9 ratio.

Differences in Tibetan Mastiffs

While the history of the breed and the breed standard speak, in general terms, of the Tibetan Mastiff, there has been great variation in size and type in the breed. When you look at some of these dogs, you may see dogs that look different from each other in style. This is because, historically, there have been different varieties of dogs in Tibet and the Himalayas labelled as "Tibetan Mastiffs." These dogs go under the names Do-khyi, Tsang Khyi, Himalayan Sheepdog, and others. These varieties were all used to save the Tibetan Mastiff after China occupied Tibet in the 1950s.

In reality, the nomads who used the Tibetan dogs – of all varieties – used different types of guardian dogs, depending on the climate and geography. Some of the varieties were more like mastiffs and other varieties were more like shepherds and mountain dogs. You can still see this in some Tibetan Mastiff bloodlines today. The major differences in the breed have come down today to the Tsang Khyi (larger, more valuable, mastiff-like) and the Do-Khyi (smaller, shepherd-like).

The largest of the Tsang Khyi dogs were often found in monasteries, given to the monks as gifts to find religious favour. Or they were sold to the wealthy to guard their courtyards. The smaller Do-Khyi dogs remained to guard flocks in the pastures, villages, and with the nomads.

When the dogs began to appear in the West, a wide range of types were sent, though you can still tell the differences, especially in size and some other traits. But bloodlines today have merged to a great extent and it becomes difficult to tell the difference between these varieties. If you have a preference (mastiff or shepherd) about the bloodline of a Tibetan Mastiff, you should talk to a breeder and be sure you know the height and weights of the puppy parents and other near relatives of the puppies. Know the bloodlines if the Tibetan Mastiff style of dog is important to you.

General facts about the Tibetan Mastiff

While the history and breed standard can give you some important information about the Tibetan Mastiff, they can't really tell you if this is a dog you can live with. Before you buy a Tibetan Mastiff puppy, you need some more facts about the breed.

Do Tibetan Mastiffs shed?

With all that massive coat, you would be wise to ask about shedding with this breed. However, as a primitive breed, the Tibetan Mastiff only has one big shed per year in the late winter or early spring. Some dogs can have a smaller shedding in the late summer or early fall. It's important to note that spaying and neutering dogs will change the coat's texture and density and can change the shedding cycle.

The breed does require regular brushing to keep their coat looking good.

Are Tibetan Mastiffs hard to train?

Yes. We are not, in any way, trying to insult these dogs or suggest that they are not intelligent. They are very intelligent. But they are independent by nature and they are not very interested in people pleasing. If you want a dog who likes to perform tricks, this is not the breed for you. Tibetan Mastiffs are simply hard to train for obedience and they are often quite stubborn.

At the same time, they are large, powerful, protective, guardian dogs and it is essential that a Tibetan Mastiff have some training and a *lot* of socialization if you are going to keep one. We'll discuss training and socialization in a later chapter.

Are Tibetan Mastiffs good with children?

Tibetan Mastiffs are good with adult-supervised children and older kids. All children should be taught to be respectful of dogs and learn how to safely interact with them. You should always be very careful about any children who may be visiting as a Tibetan Mastiff may see them as a threat.

Do Tibetan Mastiffs get along with other pets?

Tibetan Mastiffs do get along well with other pets, especially if they grow up with them from the time they are a puppy. They may have a harder time accepting a new pet in the household when they are older. Their role in life is to guard the home and its animals, so, with a little care, you should be able to introduce a new pet.

The Tibetan Mastiff as a watchdog

Obviously, the Tibetan Mastiff has been a guardian for thousands of years. Translating your dog's instincts to modern life can take a little thought and planning

First, if you have a Tibetan Mastiff, it's essential that you have a fenced yard. While the Tibetan Mastiff isn't usually inclined to roaming, you do not want your dog patrolling the neighbourhood at night or chasing a jogger three blocks. It's all too easy for your dog to inadvertently hurt someone or to be hit by a car. Because of their physical size, six-foot fences – or taller – are recommended for Tibetan Mastiffs to help deter a desire to go exploring.

Second, Tibetan Mastiffs tend to be protective of their families and territorial. It's very important for you to train your dog from a young age and spend plenty of time socializing your dog. Socialization is important for all dogs, but it's especially important for a large guardian breed that will be suspicious of anyone who comes near your home. As soon as you get a Tibetan Mastiff puppy, sign up for puppy preschool and start thinking about obedience training. Take your puppy places where you can introduce him to friendly strangers who will pet him and give him a treat. With this breed, this kind of socialization may need to continue periodically throughout your dog's life. Give him socialization refresher weeks to remind him that people are nice and we like them.

Finally, whenever you have people at your house – whether it's a repair person or a guest for a party – go out of your way to have them meet your Tibetan Mastiff. Ask them to give him a pat and a treat. Show your dog that this person is welcome in your home. Your dog may still be suspicious of them, but it will probably help him relax a little while he watches them.

Do Tibetan Mastiffs do well in all climates?

In theory, yes, Tibetan Mastiffs do well in all climates. In warm weather their undercoat will get sparser and they won't have as much coat. In reality, the Tibetan Mastiff does not do as well in very hot, humid conditions. They can live in warmer climates but if they do, they should, ideally, have access to air conditioning in the summer. Tibetan Mastiffs who live in very humid climates can have issues with fungal skin and ear infections. Dry heat is more acceptable to them. They enjoy cold weather climates best.

If you do live in a hotter climate, you can expect your Tibetan Mastiff to become lethargic in temperatures over 80 degrees Fahrenheit and his food consumption to drop 25 to 50 percent in this kind of heat.

How much do Tibetan Mastiffs cost?

In the United States you can expect to pay somewhere around $3500-4000 USD for a registered Tibetan Mastiff puppy. In the UK, the starting price is around £1,000 for a puppy. Elsewhere in the world, fabulous prices have been paid for Tibetan Mastiffs in China, though some sources claim that the prices have been inflated as breeders try to drum up interest in the dogs, as well as their cost.

As with many rare breeds, you may have to wait for a puppy. There are few Tibetan Mastiff litters born each year and puppies are usually spoken for before they are born, especially from well-known breeders.

Living arrangements for Tibetan Mastiffs

As you might guess, Tibetan Mastiffs do not do very well as apartment dogs. However, they can be very happy living in a house with a medium-sized yard. They don't require a huge area. While they do need about an hour of exercise per day, they are usually quiet in the house.

The breed enjoys routine and familiarity. They are sensitive dogs. They don't like arguments or raised voices. They would not be a good dog for someone who moves frequently or who has a lot of disruptions in their life. They need a secure home so they don't become over-protective.

Chapter Three: The Personality of the Tibetan Mastiff

As we've already said, you can expect the Tibetan Mastiff to be an independent dog. He is not wilfully disobedient but he often has his own way of doing things. He has his own agenda and he may not listen to you until he has done what *he* thinks he should do.

The Tibetan Mastiff is a confident, loyal, and reliable protector of the family. They have a strong desire to keep their home and territory safe.

Some Tibetan Mastiffs do bark quite a bit as they warn off people and animals from what they consider to be their territory. This is one of the reasons why this breed is not recommended for apartment living. Barking was considered a desirable behaviour for a guardian dog in Tibet, but it's less desirable in the suburbs.

Tibetan Mastiffs do have a noble nature and they expect to be treated like a companion. You can't simply leave one of these dogs outside and forget about him. If they become bored, indoors or outdoors, Tibetan Mastiffs are large and powerful enough to cause a tremendous amount of destruction and mischief. They can escape your yard and go looking for something interesting. Left indoors without enough attention, they can destroy your home.

This breed has enjoyed a particularly close relationship with humans over the centuries and they have a great deal of understanding. They may not always choose to obey you, but they understand a great deal. Tibetan Mastiffs are fearless dogs with initiative and controlled strength. They are patient, loyal, and gentle to those they love.

Both males and females have stable, reliable temperaments. In general, the sexes have the same differences that you find in other breeds. Male Tibetan Mastiffs can be more carefree while female Tibetan Mastiffs can be more focused on the home and family. Both sexes are devoted to the family and quite affectionate but they express their feelings differently. Males and females make equally good pets.

Tibetan Mastiffs are very pack-oriented and they enjoy spending time with their families. They are good with children, but it's important for small children to always be supervised by an adult. Accidents can happen very quickly, so don't leave small children alone with dogs. Your dog should enjoy spending time with older children.

Most of us have to work during the day and leave a dog alone for a while. Your Tibetan Mastiff should be fine if you leave him with some toys and something safe to chew on. He will probably sleep most of the day. However, it is vital that your dog spend some quality time with you and your family every day. Your Tibetan Mastiff is a pack animal and he needs to feel part of the pack – part of your family. Regular interaction with you and your family members is important. Otherwise your dog can become lonely and bored which leads to neurotic and destructive behaviour problems.

Chapter Four: Finding A Tibetan Mastiff

Finding a Tibetan Mastiff breeder is not particularly difficult. We have included a list of Tibetan Mastiff breeders in the Resources chapter later in the book to help you. However, finding a Tibetan Mastiff puppy for sale can be harder. In both the United States and the UK, this is a relatively rare breed. Although it's not unusual for Tibetan Mastiffs to have a large litter, there simply aren't many people breeding these dogs.

You may get lucky and find a puppy right away. If you don't find a Tibetan Mastiff puppy for sale immediately, or you don't find a breeder you like, don't give up. Keep checking with breeders and talking to them. Even if a breeder doesn't currently have a litter, they could be planning a litter in the next few months. Knowing a good breeder puts you on the inside track to getting the puppy you want when one is available. It's not unusual to be put on a waiting list for a pedigreed puppy in many breeds.

It's always important to talk to the breeder, not just to get information about the puppies, but to find out if this is a person you can trust.

Finding a breeder

Finding a Tibetan Mastiff breeder can be a difficult task because Tibetan Mastiffs are a rare breed. While they are starting to gain some popularity, they are still few and far between. What this means is that you may have to travel several days or have a puppy shipped to you.

In addition, it also means that you could be looking at a waiting list of up to two years before you have a puppy. This can be frustrating when you are excited about a puppy but the wait is worth it.

We have compiled a list at the back of the book with Tibetan Mastiff breeders. This is a good place to start but you should also contact the breed club, which is also listed in the resources pages.

It is important to note that you should do your research on all of the breeders listed. The priorities of breeders can change and where one was excellent at one time, they may not be currently.

When you are looking for a breeder, it is important to look for the following traits:

A breeder who will answer questions

One of the first things to look for with regard to breeders is to look for one that will answer your questions. Yes, breeders can be very busy. Not only do most of them have full time jobs and family commitments but they may also have puppies they are caring for.

However, with that being said, the breeder should be open to discussing the breed with you and potentially owning a puppy. If it is all about putting in a deposit to hold a future puppy and nothing else, then you should choose a different breeder.

A breeder who is active with the breed club and kennel club

Does the breeder register her puppies? Is she a member of the Tibetan Mastiff breed club? If the breeder answers yes to both, then you can start to feel confident with them.

A breeder who does things with her dogs

Make sure your Tibetan Mastiff breeder does something with her dogs. They don't have to show, although that would be a good option, but they do need to do more than simply place the dogs in a kennel.

A breeder who can give you backgrounds on her dogs

Choose a breeder that knows the background of her dogs such as pedigree, health of the lines and where the dogs came from. The breeder should also know the history of the breed and the breed standard.

If the breeder doesn't know much about the breed, then it is an indication that you should look elsewhere.

A breeder who has a puppy plan and health clearances

Finally, look for a breeder who has a breeding plan for her overall kennel. Is she trying to breed a certain trait or just breeding for puppies. Does she have a puppy plan on how they are raised? Does she have health clearances on her dogs? Can she talk to you knowledgeably about socialization and temperament?

If the answer is no to one or more of those questions, choose a different breeder. Every litter should have a goal in mind that will further the breed. In addition, she should have a plan as to how the puppies will be socialized and reared.

Finally, the breeder should have dogs with their health clearances. In the United States these clearances include:

- Eyes Certified by a board-certified ACVO Ophthalmologist
- OFA or PennHip certification for Hip Dysplasia
- OFA evaluation for Autoimmune Thyroiditis

OFA evaluation for elbow dysplasia is optional in the breed.

Hold every breeder you contact to those standards and this will help narrow down a breeder for you. In addition to finding these traits in a breeder, you should also look for the following.

Clean facilities

Go to the kennel if you are able to and make sure that it is clean. If you have a breeder who will not let you see the dogs or go to the kennel, choose a different breeder. The only exception to this rule is when the breeder has young puppies in the kennel, under 4 to 5 weeks of age. At this age some breeders will refuse to allow visitors because disease is easily spread to puppies and they can die.

However, if there are no litters, you should be able to go and see the Tibetan Mastiffs. When you get there, check to make sure the home, kennel and grounds are clean. If you notice a lot of dirt, or the dogs are kept in poor conditions, choose a different breeder.

Puppies that come from a dirty, poorly managed kennel can have many health and behavioural problems.

Healthy dogs

You can use this same checklist for the adult dogs in the kennel. Remember that nursing mothers will look a little rough, especially if they are nursing a large litter. Often nursing mothers will lose weight and hair and this is completely normal.

However, the rest of the dogs should look healthy and they should have good energy. It is important not to look at just the parents of the puppies but all the dogs. If any dog looks unwell, question the breeder about it.

Paperwork

Another important thing to look for is whether there is paperwork. The breeder should have a purchase contract for new puppy owners. In addition, they should have pedigree information, certification and the health clearances for their dogs. They should have registration materials. If they don't, choose a different breeder.

Puppies raised indoors

While the Tibetan Mastiff does enjoy time outside, it is important for socialization and health for all puppies to be raised in the home. Puppies raised underfoot will be the most socialized puppies and this will only be a benefit to you as the pet owner.

Good references

Finally, make sure that the breeder has excellent references.

Remember, when you are choosing your Tibetan Mastiff breeder that if you get any negative feelings from the breeder, you should find a different one.

What the breeder expects of you

At the same time, you can expect a breeder to be sizing you up, asking you questions, and checking out your references. Dog breeders put a lot of time, effort, and money, not to mention their love for their dogs, into breeding a litter of puppies. It can take years to plan a breeding and produce a litter of puppies. They are often very choosy about who they allow to buy a puppy. If the breeder gets any negative feelings about you, they have every right to refuse to sell you a puppy. It's not simply a question of going to see the nice puppies and picking out the one you want. You have to convince the breeder that you will provide a wonderful home for one of their puppies. The breeder may have a questionnaire for you. She may want to visit your home and talk to your veterinary references. Be prepared to talk to the breeder and answer some questions.

There is also some misunderstanding between the general public and dog breeders about how the Internet functions. The public believes, with some justification, that if you have a web site and show pictures of your dogs and puppies, that you are operating a business and it's okay to ask the price. Many dog breeders, especially people who breed for dog shows and as a hobby, have web sites so they can show off their dogs. They like to show pictures of their dogs the way proud parents show pictures of their kids. They may have a litter of puppies occasionally but when they get an e-mail from a stranger asking, "How much?" they are a) offended and b) suspicious. They think the person wants to do something terrible to their precious puppies like send them to a puppy farm. They will usually ignore that kind of message or send an outraged reply. Yet these are exactly the breeders who do have the best quality puppies.

If you want to contact a show or hobby breeder and inquire about a litter of puppies, it is important to follow the social niceties. Do *not* begin by asking the price. Tell the breeder that you are interested in a puppy. Tell them that you are looking for a pet (if you want a pet) or a show quality puppy if you intend to show the dog. Ask them if they have any puppies. Tell them why you like the dogs. Be candid with the breeder. Experienced breeders can tell when someone is lying to them. Just be honest. But take the time to exchange some messages with the breeder and show a real interest in the puppies instead of bluntly asking the price. Breeders can often work out different kinds of arrangements with someone if they believe the person would provide a good home for one of their puppies. Really loving the breed and the dogs goes a long way.

Adopting an Older Tibetan Mastiff

Although much of this chapter is focused on finding a Tibetan Mastiff puppy, it is important to touch on choosing an adult Tibetan Mastiff. While it is not common, it is possible to find an older Tibetan Mastiff. This can be a retired dog from a breeding kennel, a rescued dog, or an older puppy that the breeder has decided not to keep.

Adopting an older Tibetan Mastiff has many advantages:

- *Housebroken:* Many adult dogs are housebroken when you adopt them so you don't have to housetrain the dog.

- *Less destructive:* This varies from dog to dog but many adult Tibetan Mastiffs are trained before they go to your home. This means they are less likely to give in to bad habits such as chewing.

- *Affectionate:* Although most Tibetan Mastiffs are affectionate, many older dogs have an almost grateful demeanour with their new owners.

- *Trainable:* The old saying, "You can't teach an old dog new tricks," is wrong and you can teach commands to old dogs. So while many adult Tibetan Mastiffs will be trained, they can always be taught new commands.

It is important to note that it does take time for an older dog to adjust to their new home and they may be withdrawn during that time. In general, it is recommended that you give the dog about one year to adjust to the change.

If you have decided on a Tibetan Mastiff rescue, contact breeders about older dogs, or Tibetan Mastiff rescue. We have included some contact information for Tibetan Mastiff rescue groups in the Appendix.

Choosing your Tibetan Mastiff

Once you have selected the breeder and the litter is born, it is time to select the puppy. In most cases the breeder will help determine which puppy is a good match for you. Breeders usually have years of experience and can tell more about a puppy's temperament. They are good at matching puppies with people.

Sometimes a breeder will give you the choice of two or three puppies. Be open about gender and colour. It will help the breeder know which puppies might suit you.

If you are looking for a show puppy, choose one that has the looks and temperament of the breed standard. If you are looking for a pet, you can choose any colour and don't have to be so worried about the breed standard.

After the selections have been narrowed down between pet and show quality puppies, you can begin your choice. When choosing your puppy, take the time to watch the puppies while they are playing together.

Look for a puppy with an even temperament. Don't believe the myth that the puppy will choose you. Often, the puppy that greets people is the most dominant in the litter. While that is not always a bad thing, if you are looking for a quieter puppy, you won't get that with the dominant puppy.

Instead, look for a puppy that looks around, assesses the situation and then comes to you. This is usually the sign of a middle of the road temperament. Not too submissive where the puppy will be fearful and not too dominant where they are too pushy.

Don't choose the shy puppy or one that hides. A shy puppy will often grow up to have some temperament problems later in life.

In addition to looking at temperament, look at the health of your puppy. You want to choose a puppy with the following traits:

- ***Alert and energetic:*** Avoid a puppy that seems lethargic. If you arrive during puppy nap time, wait until the Tibetan Mastiff puppies are awake.

- ***Bright Eyes:*** Eyes should be clear of any debris and should not have any discharge. The Tibetan Mastiff should have bright, shiny eyes.

- ***Excellent Body Condition:*** Look at the overall condition of the body and coat. Coat should be thick and soft without crusty areas, dandruff, or dullness. The overall body of the puppy should be fat enough where you can't see the ribs but skinny enough that you can feel them when you touch his sides.

- ***Nose:*** Nose should be shiny and wet. In addition, the puppy should have no problems breathing.

- ***Excellent Sight and Hearing:*** Clap your hands, encourage the puppy to chase toys and watch his reaction. If you see any signs that he can't hear or see, you may want to choose a different puppy.

Although you will be focused on your main choice of puppy, it is important to watch all of the puppies. If you notice signs of disease in the puppies, choose a different breeder or litter.

Other traits that you should look for are a puppy that doesn't mind being touched and handled. If the puppy struggles or becomes fearful, you may want to discuss a different pick with your breeder.

Taking your time with the puppies, and visiting them more than once if you can, will help in choosing the right puppy for you. Remember to use the input of the breeder and be sure to follow your instincts as well.

In the end, this will be a relationship that lasts a lifetime so make sure it is the right one for you and your puppy from the start.

Chapter Five: Getting Ready For Your Puppy

Getting a puppy is always exciting and part of that excitement comes from everything you need to purchase for your puppy. While every dog owner is different, there are some common supplies that you should purchase for your Tibetan Mastiff.

It is important to note that the list of supplies you need for a puppy is pretty basic and you don't need to purchase everything that is recommended by your pet store. In this chapter, we'll look at the supplies that are absolute necessities and supplies that are optional. We'll also look at ways for you to puppy proof your home.

General Supplies

You don't really need a lot of things when you are getting started with your puppy. However, it is important to have your supplies before you bring your puppy home. You want to have bowls and puppy food ready before you need them, for example. And it's best not to take your puppy shopping with you before he has his vaccinations.

Supplies that you should have for your puppy are:

Feeding Bowls

Make sure that you have a water and food bowl that your puppy can reach easily. Stainless steel bowls are best. They are more durable, they don't break, they are easy to clean, and they don't allow bacteria to grow. Ceramic bowls are also a good choice, provided they are dishwasher safe. However, if they crack they can allow bacteria to grow. Plastic bowls are not a good choice. Some dogs can be allergic to the plastic and it will cause a reaction on their nose and muzzle. Scratches on the plastic can also harbour bacteria.

Collar

Purchase a flat collar for your Tibetan Mastiff puppy that will fit him when he comes home. Puppies grow quickly so most people purchase a nylon collar for a young puppy instead of purchasing expensive collars that will quickly be outgrown. The general rule is to get a collar that will allow you to put two fingers between the collar and your puppy's throat. That should be comfortable for your puppy to wear.

Leash

A 6-foot flat leash is a good choice for a puppy the size of a Tibetan Mastiff. You can easily get a leash that matches your puppy's collar. Remember to use a leash that is comfortable in your hand as well as sturdy. Although you won't need it right away, you may want to purchase a 20-foot lead for teaching the "come" command later.

You can find feeding bowls, collar, and leash at your local pet store or check online if you are buying them in advance.

Dog Grooming Items

Tibetan Mastiffs don't require a lot of grooming but they do need to be brushed regularly. While you don't need every type of dog grooming item out there, it is important to have the minimum items for grooming. These include:

- Undercoat Brush
- Brush for Long Hair
- Slicker Brush
- Nail Clippers
- Styptic Powder
- Toothbrush and Toothpaste
- Dog Shampoo
- Dog Conditioner

Most pet stores don't have a good selection of grooming tools, but you can find some of these basic implements at the pet store, especially if it's a pet super store. You may need to check online to find some grooming tools. This is especially true if you want to find a good selection of dog shampoos and conditioners.

Crate

A crate is a good idea for a Tibetan Mastiff. While some people don't like them, they are very helpful during housetraining. In addition, it will keep your puppy safe when you can't watch him or are out. Crates are *not* puppy jail. They are a den for dogs and most puppies and dogs enjoy spending time in them. They provide a good place to relax and sleep.

A Tibetan Mastiff will need a very large crate. When you are choosing a crate for your Tibetan Mastiff puppy you should keep in mind that your puppy is going to grow. Buy the crate for the size your puppy is going to be as an adult dog. You can easily buy crate "dividers" to make the crate smaller for your puppy. This will keep it the right size while your puppy is growing.

The general rule of thumb is to purchase a crate where your full grown dog can stand up in it and turn around without a problem. It should also have enough room for him to lie down comfortably.

One word of caution with crates is to never crate a dog with his collar on. It is quite easy for the dog's collar to catch on the crate bars and choke the dog.

There are lots of different kinds of crates. You can choose a hard plastic crate that is used for airline travel. These crates are a good choice if you travel with your dog in your personal vehicle since they provide protection. Or you can choose a wire crate. These crates are lightweight and easy to fold up and carry. They are a good choice for people who go to shows, obedience trials, and other events. You can also choose a canvas crate – though these are not recommended for dogs who like to use their claws to tear their way out of things.

Toys

Toys are not optional for puppies and dogs. They are a necessity. When your puppy begins chewing on something, you can reach for a toy and distract your Tibetan Mastiff from chewing. If you have ever had a puppy chew your woodwork or furniture, you know that it's much better to spend a little money on toys to entertain your puppy than spend a lot of money repairing your living room.

Make sure you choose toys that are recommended for your dog's breed and size. Yes, they even make puppy toys big enough for Tibetan Mastiff puppies. Also, choose puppy toys made for puppies to chew on them. Puppy teeth are sharp and can quickly chew through many toys if they are not made for chewing. The pieces can shred from some toys and bones and can become choking hazards. Choose puppy chew toys that are made with puppy safety in mind.

Cleaning Supplies

While not really a puppy item, cleaning supplies are necessary for bringing a puppy home. Purchase carpet and floor cleaners with enzymes to prevent further soiling.

Also, stock up on paper towels. You'll need them.

Dog Bed

Finally, purchase a dog bed or a crate bed for your puppy. Even if you allow your puppy up on the furniture, it is good to have something for him to lay on in the crate. A soft faux sheepskin mat is popular with many owners and their dogs. Or, you can use some comfy blankets.

Additional Supplies

In addition to general supplies that you will need for your puppy, there are a few additional supplies that you can get. Remember, these are optional supplies and you should only get them if you feel it is necessary.

Puppy Training Pads

These are pads that you put out for your puppy to potty. They can be used indoors or outdoors. Some people believe they make potty training easier. They are lots better than using newspapers if your puppy or dog potties indoors. They have a plastic lining on the bottom to keep liquid from spilling through and a special chemical to encourage your puppy to use them. With a dog the size of a Tibetan Mastiff you will probably want to train him to potty outside, but puppy training pads can be helpful in the early stages of housetraining.

Baby Gates

Baby gates, or pet gates, are a good choice if you want to close off rooms of your house when your puppy comes home. Once your puppy is older and more trustworthy in the house (i.e., he won't eat the buttons off your clothes), you can put the baby gates away if you like. Some people use them all the time to keep dogs out of certain parts of the house.

Stress Reducing Items

Some people like stress reducing blankets, toys and sprays for puppies, however, you probably don't need to spend this money. Instead of purchasing these items, simply take a small doggie blanket to the breeder's home and have her rub it on mother and siblings. That will provide your puppy with the same comfort.

Vitamins

While there can be benefits to giving an adult or senior dog vitamins or supplements, you should never do it without the direction of your vet. Some vitamins are toxic when given in high doses so you want to avoid inadvertently poisoning your Tibetan Mastiff. Giving vitamins and supplements to puppies is **not** advised. Puppy foods today have balanced vitamins and minerals for proper growth. Giving your puppy additional vitamins and minerals can cause musculoskeletal problems later. This is particularly true with giant breeds such as the Tibetan Mastiff.

When you are choosing your puppy supplies, take your time and start with the essentials, as well as food and treats. After that, anything else is just an added way to spoil your puppy.

Puppy Proofing your Home

Puppy proofing your home is a good way to ensure you and your Tibetan Mastiff get off to a good start together. Otherwise he could cheerfully destroy your house while he investigates it.

To prevent that destruction, it is important to puppy proof your home before your Tibetan Mastiff comes home. To properly puppy proof your home, follow the tips below.

Put up any hazardous items

Pick up and lock away any items that can be hazardous to your Tibetan Mastiff. These include:

- Household Cleaners
- Vitamins
- Medication

- Vehicle Fluids, such as antifreeze
- Salts for Ice or Water softener
- Pool Chemicals
- Tobacco Products

Puppy's eye view

Take the time to crawl around your home before your puppy arrives and then once or twice a week. Look at things from your puppy's vantage point. Pick up small clips, tags, paper, anything that can be a choking hazard for puppy.

Also, keep clothes picked up. It can be surprising but some articles of clothing, such as socks, can pose a choking hazard for your Tibetan Mastiff.

Put knick-knacks up high

While you may love having your ornaments on tables and shelves, look at what your Tibetan Mastiff can reach. If he can get it, move it up out of reach. Wagging tails have a way of knocking everything off a coffee table. Puppies also like to explore by putting things in their mouths. Putting your objects away will prevent the item from being broken and your puppy from getting hurt. It doesn't have to be permanent but only until your Tibetan Mastiff learns what he is and is not allowed to touch.

Close off access to standing water

Close toilet seat lids, drain tubs and sinks, and block off any access to a pool if you have one. Standing water can be very tempting for a Tibetan Mastiff. However, young puppies cannot swim or swim well and falling into the water could lead to a drowning.

Tie up those electrical cords and drapery cords

Electrical cords are always very tempting for a puppy and are often chewed. Always tape your cords out of reach of your puppy. Also, look for cords that dangle from furniture as the puppy may knock a lamp down on himself while playing with a cord.

Don't forget about computer and phone cords. Make sure they are tucked away, if possible.

In addition to electrical cords, pull up the drape or blind cords. These can lead to strangulation if the puppy gets caught in them.

Keep garbage out of reach or in a puppy proof container

Another tempting item for puppies is the garbage can. Always keep it put up where the puppy can't get at it and make sure you empty it every night, especially if your puppy isn't sleeping in his crate.

Block off stairs

Even if you allow your Tibetan Mastiff upstairs with you, block off the stairs at both the top and the bottom. Puppies do not have a lot of coordination and taking stairs can be difficult for them. It is quite common for a puppy to fall down stairs. To prevent this, keep the stairs blocked and off limits.

Keep doors closed

Any door or window leading to the outside should be kept closed if the puppy can access it. An open door can be irresistible for a puppy.

Check the outdoors

In addition to puppy proofing your house, make sure that you check the outdoors. Look for openings in the fence and items that can be hazardous to your Tibetan Mastiff puppy. If there are any drainpipes, pools, or other items in your yard, they can present a risk.

If you find anything, pick up all the hazardous items and fence or block off the rest, such as the pool or drain pipes. The goal is to make the outdoors as safe as the indoors.

Look at your plants

Finally, look at the plants that you have in your home and garden. Many plants are poisonous to dogs so avoid having them in your home. If you do have them, make sure they are in areas where your puppy cannot reach them.

In the end, puppy proofing is simply keeping your house neat and tidy – and taking a few precautions. Everyone in the home should work with you to keep the space clean and you should constantly reassess if your house is still safe for your puppy.

Staying on top of puppy proofing will keep your puppy safe.

Toxic Plants

Here is a list of plants that you should avoid having both outside and in. All of the plants on this list are poisonous in varying degrees to your Tibetan Mastiff.

Aconite	Emerald Feather	Nightshade
Aloe Vera	English Ivy	Oaks
Amaryllis	Eucalyptus	Oleander
Apple Leaf Croton	European Bittersweet	Onions
Arrowgrasses	False Fax	Oriental Lily
Asparagus Fern	False Hellebore	Peace Lily
Atropa belladonna	Fan Weed	Peach Tree
Autumn Crocus	Fiddle-leaf Fig	Pencil Cactus
Azalea	Field Peppergrass	Philodendrons
Baby's Breath	Florida Beauty	Plumosa Fern
Baneberry	Foxglove	Pokeweed
Bird of Paradise	Fruit Salad Plant	Poinsettia
Black Locust	Geranium	Poison Hemlock
Bloodroot	German Ivy	Poison Ivy
Box	Giant Dumb Cane	Poison Oak
Branching Ivy	Glacier Ivy	Potato Plant
Buckeye	Gold Dust Dracaena	Pothos
Buddhist Pine	Golden Pothos	Precatory Bean
Buttercup	Hahn's Self-Branching Ivy	Primrose
Caladium	Heartland Philodendron	Rattle box
Calla Lily	Holly	Red Emerald

Carolina Jessamine	Horsechestnut	Red Princess
Castor Bean	Horse Nettle	Red-Margined Dracaena
Ceriman	Hurrican Plant	Rhododendron
Charming Dieffenbachia	Indian Rubber Plant	Rhubarb
Cherry Tree	Iris	Ribbon Plant
Chinaberry Tree	Jack-in-the-Pulpit	Rosary Pea
Chinese Evergreen	Japanese Show Lily	Saddle Leaf Philodendron
Chockcherries	Jatropha	Sago Palm
Christmas Berry	Jerusalem Cherry	Satin Pothos

Chapter Six: Bringing Your Tibetan Mastiff Puppy Home

So you have selected your puppy, purchased the supplies and waited the long weeks before your puppy comes home. This is always an exciting time but it's important to remember that picking your Tibetan Mastiff puppy up is just as important as caring for him later. That's because your puppy's introduction to your home and family can affect his development and the bond you develop later.

In this chapter, we'll go over everything you need to know about bringing your Tibetan Mastiff puppy home.

The Day of Pick Up

The day you pick up your Tibetan Mastiff puppy is always exciting. If you haven't been lucky enough to find a breeder with puppies, it can mean that you have waited months or even years to get your puppy. It can be difficult to stay calm but it is important to do so for the sake of your puppy. Puppies are often nervous and scared during this time of transition. When you are calm, it is reassuring to your puppy.

You can begin taking steps to make the transition go smoothly before you even arrive at the breeder's house. If possible, send a blanket to the breeder a few days ahead of time and ask her to rub it on your puppy's siblings and mother. If it isn't possible, bring the blanket with you when you pick him up. Your puppy can start to become accustomed to your scent and associate it with the comforting smells of his current family.

In some cases you may be picking up a puppy at the airport,

especially if you have found a breeder who lives a long distance from you. If this is the case, then you and the breeder should discuss everything over the phone ahead of time. The breeder should have the puppy's vaccination records and health certificate, as well as his other travel papers so he can fly. A puppy as large as a Tibetan Mastiff puppy usually has to fly as cargo – even when they are 8-12 weeks old, they are usually too large to fit in a carry-on bag and fly in the cabin.

You will need to make sure that you have all of the puppy's travel information from the breeder so you know where and when the puppy is arriving. Different airlines handle shipping dogs in different ways, so it's a good idea to call the airline ahead of time and make sure you have the details correct. Cargo offices are not always open 24 hours a day, so make sure you will be able to pick up your puppy right after the plane arrives.

Resist the temptation to open your puppy's crate door as soon as you see him at the airport. Dogs can and do get lost at airports. Wait until you have the crate safely secured in your vehicle before you open the door. Once you have your puppy's collar and leash on, you can stop at a rest area and let him potty and give him some fresh water.

It's usually best if you leave your children at home when you pick up your new Tibetan Mastiff puppy. This is true whether you are picking the puppy up at the breeder's home or going to the airport. While it's a good idea to discuss your children with the breeder so she can help you choose which puppy is best-suited to live with kids, bringing the puppy home can be a stressful time for your Tibetan Mastiff and the excitement of children can make it more so. Before you leave to get the puppy, have everything set up for him so you can simply bring him home and take him to his safe place.

If you are picking your puppy up at the breeder's house, place a crate in your car for your Tibetan Mastiff to travel home in. Puppies should never sit in the driver's lap or be loose in the car. It is much too easy for a puppy to distract the driver and cause an accident.

Once you arrive at the breeder's house, spend some time with your puppy, his littermates, his mother, and with the breeder. If you have some last minute questions, try to have them written down so you won't forget them. Building a good relationship with your puppy's breeder is important. She will be a valuable resource for you throughout your puppy's life.

After you leave the breeder's home, you should go straight home. Don't stop to visit a friend or go to a pet store. Every place you stop can expose your Tibetan Mastiff puppy to disease at this age and to extra stress. Try to keep your puppy calm and don't worry. Your puppy will soon be able to visit friends and go places with you.

Keep an eye on your Tibetan Mastiff puppy in the car. Many puppies experience motion sickness in cars. It's possible that your puppy has already taken some car trips to the vet, but some puppies will still get car sick. If you see your puppy's nose drooping towards the floor, or drooling and wrinkling his lips, pull over and allow him time to get over his car sickness. He may throw up but that is perfectly normal. It's a good idea to take some paper towels and cleaner with you. This is another reason why we recommend crating your puppy on the ride home. It's easier to clean the crate if your puppy becomes sick than to have to try to clean your entire car.

If you do have to stop, whether for a potty break or because your puppy is car sick, try to stop at secluded spots where you won't see a lot of dogs. Take him to an area to potty and then immediately pick him up. Avoid other dogs as you don't know which ones have been properly vaccinated.

When you get home, immediately take your puppy outside to potty. Puppies will usually sniff around the yard and then relieve themselves. Once your puppy has relieved himself, you can enter the house and go to a quiet room together.

Sit with your Tibetan Mastiff puppy and allow him the opportunity to explore his surroundings. Some Tibetan Mastiff puppies will want to play and run around, others will want to sleep. Follow your puppy's cues.

You can introduce your puppy slowly to family members. Keep all interactions with the new puppy calm. During the first few days you will find your Tibetan Mastiff sleeps a lot. This is normal for all puppies at a young age. However, this will change as he becomes familiar with his home and as he gets older and gains confidence.

As far as house rules are concerned, you should start the way you mean to continue. Keep to a schedule for housetraining and stick to rules. A schedule will help your puppy know when and where he is supposed to potty. If your Tibetan Mastiff will not be allowed on the furniture when he is a large adult dog, don't let him up when he is a cute puppy.

Keep your puppy confined to one area and then slowly open up your home to your puppy as he becomes more confident and trustworthy. In reality, the key to introducing your puppy to his new home is in being calm, progressing slowly, and creating those rules and schedules.

Introducing your Tibetan Mastiff to other family members

Once your puppy is home, it's time to introduce him to the other residents in your home. While your first instinct is probably to rush in and introduce him to everyone, your Tibetan Mastiff can become very frightened or overwhelmed by too much attention all at once. A puppy can withdraw and shut down if he is overwhelmed by his surroundings or by meeting too many people.

Since you want all introductions to be positive, it's best to make the introductions as calmly as possible. Let your puppy have time to get used to his new home.

One of the best things that you can do for your puppy when you bring him home is to allow him to rest in a quiet room. After he has had some time to adjust, start bringing in people to meet him, one at a time.

Other animals in the home can wait a day or two. There is no rush and you want to do the introductions properly to prevent any lasting problems for your Tibetan Mastiff.

Children

For younger children, it's a good idea to introduce them to your Tibetan Mastiff puppy one at a time. This will help minimize the amount of stimulation the puppy has. If you have older children, you can introduce them together.

When you are introducing your Tibetan Mastiff puppy to children, start by having your child come into the room and sit down on the floor. Don't rush the puppy or place the puppy in your child's lap.

Instead, give the child treats to feed the puppy and allow the puppy to approach on his own terms. Tell the child to stay calm and quiet so the puppy won't get frightened.

Tibetan Mastiffs have a natural fondness for children so your puppy should gravitate to the child. When the puppy does greet the child, let the child pet the Tibetan Mastiff calmly.

Keep meetings short and build up their length. In addition, over the first few days, make all interactions with the children calm and quiet. As the puppy gets used to the sounds of children, you can start introducing play times.

It's important that children should have rules regarding the puppy and they should be taught how to treat the dog. Make sure your children understand the following rules:

- Be calm around the puppy.
- Don't hold onto him when he wants to go.
- Never hit or pinch the puppy.
- Don't pull on ears or tail.
- Gently pet the puppy.
- Use toys to play with the puppy.
- Don't try to take toys or food away from a puppy or dog.
- Don't run away from a puppy or dog.

Unfortunately, most puppies and dogs don't respect children the same way they do the adult (taller) members of the family. Your children won't be able to command your puppy with the same authority that you have until they are a little older. It's important that an adult is always present to supervise when small children play with puppies and dogs to keep accidents from happening. Once your children are a little older, your dog will respect them more and play is less likely to get out of hand.

As you train your Tibetan Mastiff puppy, you should include your children in the puppy's training and socialization. This will be helpful for both your puppy and your children in the long run.

Other Pets

Introducing your Tibetan Mastiff puppy to other pets in the home is something that you should do gradually. Remember that the animals in the home were there first and they can have some behavioural problems with a new puppy such as jealousy or problems with territory.

To prevent these problems, make sure that you make the meetings short and that you do not force any relationships. The animals in your home will sort out their hierarchy on their own.

When introducing other pets, it is important to follow these rules:

Keep your puppy confined
The first rule is that you should always keep your puppy confined when you bring him home. Place your Tibetan Mastiff in a quiet room. This will keep your puppy safe while still making your current pet feel confident.

When you are bringing the puppy out of his room, confine the current dog unless you are taking the time to introduce them.

Allow door sniffing
Or crate sniffing. What this means is that you should allow your current pet to sniff at the crate or the door where the puppy is. Don't let them be pushy and if your puppy starts to look stressed, stop the behaviour.

Sniffing at the door will help your pet become acquainted with the puppy while there is a safe barrier between the pet and the puppy.

Set up the meeting
Plan meetings between your current pet and your puppy in advance. Never bring in a puppy and then allow your current pet to take charge. Instead, wait until your current pet is calm before you make the introductions. This will help promote a positive experience for both your new Tibetan Mastiff and your current pet.

Encourage your current pet to equate your puppy with positives
When you are doing the introductions, always provide your current pet with plenty of affection. Give him lots of praise for greeting nicely and make sure that you give him plenty of treats. The more you praise your current pet, the more he will think the new Tibetan Mastiff puppy is something positive.

Let cats greet on their own terms
While you can control the meetings between a dog and puppy, it can be difficult to control the meeting between a puppy and cat. Often, puppies find cats interesting (too interesting) and will try to chase the cat or play with him. When this happens, the cat will usually react.

The best thing to do is to allow the cat to watch the Tibetan

Mastiff puppy from his own vantage points. Praise, treat, and pet the cat when you are able so he will be comfortable with the new excitement in the home.

After a few weeks, start bringing your cat down from his perches, but only when the puppy is calm. Do not introduce the cat in the middle of a play session. Always make sure that you have control of your Tibetan Mastiff puppy to prevent him from chasing the cat.

It may take time but eventually your Tibetan Mastiff will come to make friends with the cat, though it will always be on the cat's terms.

Make the older pet the primary pet
What this means is that your current pet should have more rights than the puppy. The current pet should be fed first, you should greet him first when you get home, and you should always allow the current pet to enter or exit first.

It may be hard to believe, but if you support your older pet's position, it shows the puppy that he must respect the older pet. You will avoid fights over status and rank if you back your older pet's rights. Your puppy may try to challenge your older pet's authority from time to time, but it's up to you to support your older pet if you want peace in your home. Occasionally there is an older dog who is happy to allow a puppy to assume leadership, but this is rare.

As the animals become more acquainted with each other, you can start offering more attention and other things equally but for the first few months, make the current pet feel extra special.

Be patient

Finally, be patient with your pets. Remember that this is a big adjustment for them and that they may not warm up quickly. In fact, many times it can take up to 6 months for the puppy to be accepted by the current pets. For cats, it can take up to a year.

Socialization and the First Few Weeks

We'll discuss socialization for your Tibetan Mastiff puppy more thoroughly a little later, but we should touch on it here. Socialization is an important aspect of your puppy's life and it actually starts from the moment he is born.

Before he even comes home with you, your breeder has probably already been socializing your puppy. Puppies that are raised in a home environment learn about vacuums, televisions, music, meet people, and get lots of love and petting from the moment they are born. Most breeders will take puppies outside to let them experience the grass and other surfaces. Puppies usually go to the vet and meet some friendly strangers there. In addition, your Tibetan Mastiff puppy's mother and littermates will also teach him puppy manners so he has some idea of how to behave with other dogs.

However, after you bring your puppy home, it is up to you to continue to socialize your Tibetan Mastiff. That's especially important with this breed which can be reserved and suspicious of people because of their flock guarding dog heritage. Many trainers will recommend puppy classes after 16 weeks of age and won't stress socialization until after those classes start. Puppy kindergarten classes are important and they are strongly recommended for the Tibetan Mastiff, but you should be socializing your puppy well before 16 weeks. The crucial time period for puppy socialization is between 7 to 9 weeks of age.

Obviously, between 3 and 8 weeks of age, your puppy will be socialized at the breeder's home. However, between 8 to 16 weeks, you need to take the time to work on socialization. The reason why this is a crucial period is because during this time, puppies are less fearful and more open to new experiences.

Between 7 and 9 weeks of age, some puppies sooner, others later, the Tibetan Mastiff puppy will start to become more cautious about new things and this can make socialization harder.

The main problem with this window is the fact that your Tibetan Mastiff cannot go to many places until he has had his second set of vaccinations. However, you can still work on socialization at home.

During the first few weeks at home, from 8 to 16 weeks, take the time to socialize your puppy to a range of different stimuli in the house. For example, continue to expose your puppy to the same things he probably experienced at the breeder's home: vacuum, watch television, and have guests over.

Make sure that you touch your puppy and handle him often so he can become socialized to your touch. After your puppy is 12 weeks old, or has had his second set of shots, take your puppy places where puppies and dogs are welcome and continue his socialization with others.

Puppies will continue to go through different stages as they grow and develop, including more fear stages.

The Critical Fear Periods in Puppies

- Seven to Nine Weeks

- Four to Six Months
- Approximately Eight to Nine Months
- Approximately Twelve Months
- Approximately Fourteen to Eighteen Months

During these stages your puppy can be fearful of people, places, and objects that he already knows. He might bark at very ordinary things. He might shake or hide from something that wouldn't normally bother him. This is all normal behavior for your puppy during these stages. Stick to familiar routines during these times. Reward positive behaviour and try not to encourage fearful behaviour.

For more information on socialization, read the chapter on socializing your Tibetan Mastiff.

Chapter Seven: Caring for your Tibetan Mastiff

Caring for your Tibetan Mastiff does not have to be something that is overly complicated. Despite the fact that they are a large dog with a lot of hair, they don't require a lot of grooming. Although they do need regular exercise, they are fairly quiet in the house.

Tibetan Mastiffs can be challenging for some owners because of their size. If you are a first-time dog owner or if you have been used to a smaller dog, then it may take some adjustment to care for a dog as large as a Tibetan Mastiff.

In this chapter, we'll go over everything you need to know about taking care of your dog on a day to day basis.

Daily Care

Setting up a daily schedule will help you to care for your Tibetan Mastiff. Remember, when the dog is young, he won't be able to be left alone for long periods. You can expect about two hours between each potty break.

As your Tibetan Mastiff gets older, you will be able to leave him for longer periods without having any problems with him having an accident in the house.

Your Tibetan Mastiff's schedule should include the following:

Feeding

Dogs should be fed every day and how often really depends on your dog's age. Puppies usually need to be fed about three times per day when they are young. As your puppy gets older, you can begin to feed him twice a day. Most breeders recommend feeding adult dogs twice a day.

You can also give your dog treats but remember that treats contribute to your dog's daily intake of calories. Too many treats can put pounds on your dog. Small treats are good to use as a reward when you are training your dog. You can use anything your dog likes as a treat. You can also use healthy treats such as carrot pieces or apple slices.

Watering

Make sure your Tibetan Mastiff always has access to fresh, clean water. Dogs typically drink more water when the weather is hot, but they should always have water available.

Grooming

Despite the heavy coat, Tibetan Mastiffs usually only have one big shed or "molt" per year. However, they do need regular brushing. The coat naturally sheds most dirt and debris. Tibetan Mastiffs are known for not having a doggy odor like most dogs.

You can expect to brush your dog several times per week and bathe as necessary. When the dog is shedding heavily, you will need to brush more often and use a deshedding tool to help remove the dead hair.

You will also need to keep your dog's nails trimmed. If this is something you are uncomfortable doing yourself, veterinarians will often cut nails for their clients or you can visit a pet groomer.

You will also need to check your dog's ears regularly to make sure they are clean. We also recommend that you brush your dog's teeth often. You can purchase a doggy toothbrush and doggy toothpaste at a pet store or online. Do not use human toothpaste. It can contain xylitol (an artificial sweetener) which is toxic to dogs.

Vaccinations

Most breeders will advise you to take your new puppy to the vet within 48 to 72 hours after bringing him home. This is good for everyone involved: you, the breeder, and the puppy. If you have a contract with the breeder, it probably has this kind of stipulation in it. It's important to make sure that the puppy is in good health when he arrives at your home. Depending on his age and where he is in his vaccination schedule, you may also be able to get his next vaccinations when you visit the vet for this check-up.

Recommended vaccinations can vary slightly, depending on where you live. Standard puppy vaccinations in Great Britain include the following:

- Canine Parvovirus
- Canine Distemper
- Canine Parainfluenza Virus
- Infectious Canine Hepatitis
- Kennel Cough
- Leptospirosis

Coronavirus is considered optional. Rabies is usually only given to dogs in the UK if they are planning a trip abroad since rabies has been eradicated in Great Britain.

Puppies receive the same vaccinations in the United States, though leptospirosis is considered optional, depending on where you live. In some areas a vaccination for Lyme disease (spread by ticks) can also be given, but it is not considered a basic vaccination. The rabies vaccine, however, is required for dogs by every state, usually by the time a puppy is four months old.

Some of these vaccines, such as the parvo vaccine, need to be given several times over the course of several weeks to make sure the puppy is fully immunized. Once your puppy's vaccinations are completed, he will need to have booster shots when he's a year old. After that, the vaccines will need to be updated every two to three years so your puppy won't need to get all of the vaccinations at the same time again.

Training and Socializing

Tibetan Mastiffs are innately reserved and can be territorial without good socialization so be sure to start socialization early and continue it throughout your dog's life.

Tibetan Mastiffs are not the easiest dogs to train. They are independent by nature. But training your dog is important. Dogs the size of a Tibetan Mastiff need to be under their owner's control. Training is also a good way to bond with your dog and it keeps your dog from getting bored.

If you spend 15 to 20 minutes per day training and socializing your puppy, you will see positive results.

Exercise

In addition to training and socializing, your Tibetan Mastiff requires exercise. Walks, playing fetch, or formal activities such as dog sports are all good ways to exercise your dog.

Bathroom Breaks

Another factor with daily care is taking your Tibetan Mastiff outside for potty breaks. When your Tibetan Mastiff is a puppy, you will need to let him out every few hours.

The general rule with puppies is that they can hold their bladder for one hour for every month of age. So with that in mind, you should expect to take your puppy outside every 2 hours when he is 8 weeks old. Bear in mind that some puppies can hold their bladder longer than others so don't use the general rule as a hard rule. Also, don't expect your puppy to be fully housetrained until he is about 6 months of age. Training will also depend on you.

With adult Tibetan Mastiffs you should expect to take your dog out 4 to 5 times a day, if not more. Most people take their dogs out as soon as they get up in the morning, after each meal, when they come home from work, and before bed. If you have your own yard, even better. You can allow your dog to spend more time outside and exercise himself.

Quality Time

Finally, you should include quality time in your schedule every day. A Tibetan Mastiff thrives when he can spend time with his owner. This doesn't have to be time-consuming but can be as simple as sitting down and petting him while you watch TV.

Take the time to make your Tibetan Mastiff happy and you will find he is a wonderful companion you love spending time with.

In the end, daily care can take you all of an hour a day and many of the things you need to do for your Tibetan Mastiff can be done when you are doing other things.

Exercise

Exercise is an important part of caring for your Tibetan Mastiff and will be one of the deciding factors in how happy your puppy is.

Tibetan Mastiffs can be somewhat deceptive in terms of their exercise requirements. As flock guardians they were most alert at night, acting as sentries. Even today, it is not unusual for these dogs to sleep all day. You may get the impression that your dog doesn't need or want much exercise. However, he will likely be awake at night, guarding the house. Tibetan Mastiffs should not be left outside at night or they have a tendency to bark at every strange sound – making you unpopular with your neighbors.

You can deter your dog's tendency to sleep all day and stay awake at night by taking him for several long walks during the day. In the case of a dog this large, your walks will need to be at least 30 minutes to give him enough exercise and make him tired enough to sleep at night. This recommendation is for adult dogs. Puppies will tired more easily. You should take them out more often and for shorter times.

As mentioned earlier, if you have a fenced garden or yard, you can encourage your dog to spend time outside exercising during the day. Do make sure that you have a tall, secure fence so your dog won't be tempted to try to escape.

It's also important to spend quality time outside with your Tibetan Mastiff. Play fetch, take him to a dog park, or simply do some training in the backyard. The key is to spend some time together outdoors bonding with your Tibetan Mastiff.

Another important aspect of exercise is to exercise your Tibetan Mastiff's mind. These are very intelligent dogs and they can become a handful when they do not have something to do. Give them access to toys when you are away. There are all kinds of toys for dogs today from simple balls and rope toys to more complex toys that challenge a dog's IQ. Provide your dog with a variety and he is sure to find some to keep him busy.

Grooming

The Tibetan Mastiff is a breed that will require regular grooming since they do have a thick coat. When they blow coat, which is another term used to describe heavy shedding, you will need to make your grooming a daily occurrence.

Although many people view grooming as a chore, it can actually be a very pleasant activity for you and your Tibetan Mastiff. It provides you with an opportunity to bond with your dog and also creates a period of quiet time for your Tibetan Mastiff.

In addition, it helps you stay on top of health problems with your dog since part of grooming is checking over their health. You can check your dog's body for any lumps or bumps that might be a cause of concern.

In addition, Tibetan Mastiffs have such thick, heavy coat that you need to keep your dog groomed in order to treat for fleas and ticks. You won't be able to apply a monthly flea preventive to keep fleas away if the coat is unkempt. If your dog already has fleas, you won't be able to apply any products to kill them if the coat is clumped and unbrushed.

It's a good idea to groom puppies daily. There isn't a lot of real grooming to do, but it's a great way to get your puppy used to being touched and handled. Take the time to touch his paws, tail, head and body. Make it a positive experience with treats and praise. If you start off in this way with your puppy, grooming will always be easy and enjoyable for you both.

Bathing

Bathing is not something that needs to be done frequently with a Tibetan Mastiff. They do not have much doggy odour and their coat tends to shed dirt, so try to avoid frequent bathing. Too much bathing can dry out the skin, removing the coat's natural oils, which will damage the coat and cause you more problems.

Bathing once every two to three months is usually more than enough to keep your Tibetan Mastiff clean. Before bathing, you should brush your Tibetan Mastiff with a slicker brush to remove any knots or hair. When bathing, use a gentle, cleansing coat shampoo for dogs. Avoid human shampoos as the many chemicals and additives to human shampoo often dry out a dog's coat. You can also use a dog coat conditioner after bathing or a detangler for dog coats.

Bathe your Tibetan Mastiff in warm water and make sure that you always rinse the coat completely. Leaving shampoo residue can lead to dandruff.

Nail Clipping

Most Tibetan Mastiffs don't like their paws to be handled, but clipping your dog's nails is another important part of regular care. Nail clipping, and the frequency of clipping, differs from dog to dog. Some dogs require their nails to be clipped once a week, others once a month. Where you live, the flooring and ground outside, and other factors, as well as the individual dog, will determine how long the nails get and how often they need to be trimmed.

To properly clip your Tibetan Mastiff's nails, you can either use a traditional clipper, which has a sharp blade or a dremel tool. Dremels, which are small sanding tools, keep the nail smooth. If the quick is cut, which is the vein in each nail, the dremel tool will cauterize the cut and prevent bleeding. However, some dogs object to the noise the dremel makes. If you plan to use a dremel on your dog's nails, it helps to begin when your dog is a puppy.

Nail clippers are easy to use but you run the risk of cutting the nail too short, which can be painful to your dog. If you cut your dog's nails too short once or twice, your dog can become foot shy and clipping his nails becomes a struggle.

When you are clipping your dog's nails, hold the paw firmly in one hand. Holding the tool at a 90 degree angle with the nail, grind or make a small cut. Never take a lot of nail off at one time. Instead, make small cuts and slowly work your way back. It's much better to trim a small amount and shorten the nails over the course of several days or weeks than try to make them too short in one session.

In dogs with clear nails, you should be able to see the quick as a pink line in the centre of the nail. In dogs with black nails, simply cut back until you start to see a grey oval in the nail. This is the main indication that you are close to the quick.

If you happen to cut the quick, don't worry. You can stop the bleeding by dipping the nail in cornstarch or styptic powder. Although your dog will yelp in pain, it is important to cut another nail on the dog before you end the session. The reason for this is so the dog does not end a nail clipping session on a negative. End every grooming session with a positive so your Tibetan Mastiff realizes that grooming is a positive thing.

We recommend giving your dog a treat and lots of praise as you trim every nail. Let your dog know that getting his nails done is something good. Be lavish with your treats and praise.

Brushing

Tibetan Mastiffs should be brushed several times per week. Brushing has a lot of benefits:

- Allows you to bond with your dog.
- Helps distribute natural oils through your dog's coat.
- Removes dead skin.
- Removes dead hair.
- Allows you an opportunity to check the health of your dog's body.

When your Tibetan Mastiff is young, it is important to spend time simply brushing and petting your puppy in a grooming session.

This will make grooming very positive for your Tibetan Mastiff and will ensure that he enjoys it. It will also give you the opportunity to look over your dog and make sure that he is healthy and happy.

To brush a Tibetan Mastiff you can use a good slicker brush followed by a good bristle brush. With this breed you will need to select brushes that have longer bristles so they can reach through the coat. Brush your dog going in the direction of hair growth, not against it. Use smaller brushes and combs for the legs and other parts of the body.

Brushing should only take 10 to 20 minutes. End every brushing session with a treat so your dog will look forward to being groomed.

Ears

Tibetan Mastiffs can be somewhat prone to ear infections so it is important to clean their ears regularly. In your dog has any kind of ear infection, you can expect to find a strong odour coming from the ears. Finding mud or other dirt on the inner ear flap is not a sign that your dog has an ear problem. Ear infections occur in the ear canal.

To clean the ears you should never stick anything inside the ear canal. For example, q-tips will often push the debris down into the ear and this will cause more problems.

You can buy ear cleaning solution for dogs from your veterinarian or at the pet store. Soak a cotton ball in the solution. Place the swab into the ear and then massage the base of the ear. Remove the swab and wipe the outside of the ear canal and the overall ear until they are clean. You can repeat this process as long as any debris or wax continues to come up from the ear canal.

Check the inside of the ears for any hair and trim or pull it if there are mats in the hair or hair growing down inside the ear canal. Keeping the ear clear of too much hair allows air to flow to the ear and discourages bacteria from growing. It's a good way to prevent ear infections.

And that is all there is to cleaning your Tibetan Mastiff's ears. Remember to never put anything down into the ears that is smaller than your finger and if you see any type of unusual discharge, take your dog to the vet.

Teeth

The final thing you should attend to for your Tibetan Mastiff are his teeth. Unlike people, dog's do not need their teeth brushed several times a day. Instead, you can brush them several times a week.

When you brush your dog's teeth, make sure that you use a canine toothbrush. If you haven't introduced your dog to brushing, start with just the toothbrush without toothpaste.

Never use human toothpaste as it can make a dog sick. Use a toothpaste made for dogs instead. You can buy toothbrushes and toothpaste made for dogs at a pet store or online. Most dogs like having their teeth brushed once they are introduced to it. Doggy toothpaste is made in flavours such as peanut butter, beef, and chicken. Dogs usually think the toothpaste is a treat.

When brushing the teeth, all you need to brush are the outside surface of the teeth. The top of each tooth, as well as the inside of the teeth, are kept clean by the dog's tongue.

And that is all you need to know about grooming your Tibetan Mastiff. While it may seem like a lot, it really is only a few minutes each day.

Training

We have mentioned the difficulty of training a Tibetan Mastiff several times. This section is about the essential commands that your Tibetan Mastiff should know and how to teach those commands to your dog.

We recommend using a small treat morsel that is soft and does not require a lot of chewing for training. Hard treats that need to be chewed break the training session too much. The dog has to focus more on chewing than on training. Hotdogs make excellent small treats. Slice the hotdogs into pieces that are no larger than your pinkie nail. These treats have tons of flavour and are easy to chew. In addition, their smell is perfect for baiting a dog into position. The dog will always follow your hand when you are holding a hot dog treat.

It's important that the bait treats are small because you don't want the dog to fill up too quickly. You need him to stay hungry enough to pay attention for the entire time you are training. On the same note, do not feed your dog a big meal just before you start to train or your dog won't be interested in your treats. In fact, he will probably feel like taking a nap.

When you are training your Tibetan Mastiff, keep him on the leash the entire time unless you are practising off-leash lessons. This will prevent him from wandering away when he is bored. (Hopefully your dog won't get bored with your lessons.)

In addition, there are always some sequences that you should follow. First, never give the command more than once. If you repeat the command, your Tibetan Mastiff will decide that he doesn't have to listen.

Second, give praise before the treat. You want your Tibetan Mastiff to be working for praise not food. Finally, always touch the dog's collar when he has completed the command.

The reason for the latter is to let the dog know that touching the collar is not bad. Often, when we give a command, such as come, sit and heel, it is because we want to gain control of them. If we don't train a dog to become familiar with having their leash touched, the dog may get into the habit of running from you when you go to grab his collar.

a. "Sit!"

"Sit" is one of the first commands your Tibetan Mastiff will need to learn. To train "sit," do the following:

1. Have your dog stand in front of you so he is facing you.

2. Place a treat in your right hand and place it near his nose. Do not let him get at the treat.

3. Give the command, never repeat the command, just say it once, "Sit."

4. Bring the treat up and over his head slowly. His muzzle should follow and his bottom should drop.

5. If he tries to step back to follow the treat, restrict his movement with the leash and repeat the action. You are either too high or

going too quickly. Do not repeat the command.

6. If he still doesn't sit, apply a small amount of pressure to his hind quarters to make his butt drop.

7. The second his bottom touches the ground in a sit, praise the dog, touch his collar and then treat.

b. "Stay!"

"Stay" is another command that is taught when your puppy is young. It is an important command that can be used in conjunction with a number of different commands. To train stay, do the following:

1. Place your dog into a sit or down position.

2. Give the dog the command, "Stay."

3. Place your hand in front of his nose, palm facing the dog.

4. Remove your hand and take a step back.

5. If he breaks the "stay," give a firm correction with your voice and place him directly back where you gave the "stay" command.

6. If he doesn't move, take a step back to him and praise, touch his collar and treat him.

7. Repeat the process, slowly going further away from him and making him wait for longer as the training progresses.

c. "Down"

Teaching "down" refers to teaching your Tibetan Mastiff to lay down. This should be taught after your dog has learned the sit command since you will often put them into a "down" from a "sit," especially when they are first learning the command. To train "down," do the following:

1. Place your dog into a "sit" in front of you so he is facing you.

2. Place a treat in your right hand and place it near his nose. Do not let him get at the treat.

3. Give the command, "Down."

4. Lower the treat to the floor between his paws and move the treat away from the dog. Move slowly so the dog will follow the treat.

5. If he tries to step forward to follow the treat, restrict his movement with the leash and repeat the action.

You are either going too quickly or moving too far forward. Do not repeat the command.

6. If he still doesn't lay down, apply a small amount of pressure to his shoulders to encourage him to lay down.

7. When he is laying down, give the dog praise, touch his collar and treat.

d. "Come"

This is one of the most important commands that you can teach your Tibetan Mastiff, and is also one of the hardest. This is the command where you will need to have some trust in your dog. However, when you are first training your Tibetan Mastiff, you will need to keep him on the leash.

When you are teaching "come," it is important to never use the command for punishment. What this means is that you should never tell your Tibetan Mastiff to "come" when he has done something wrong, and then punish him when he does. The dog will learn that "come" is a bad thing and he won't come at any other time.

Instead, make it the most wonderful thing that your dog can do. Heap praise on him and give him lots of treats. To encourage your Tibetan Mastiff to come, clap your hands, be exciting and interesting and your Tibetan Mastiff will come running.

You can train "come" in two different ways, one is when you place him in a "sit" and "stay," and then call him to "come." This is a focused "come" and while it is useful, it shouldn't be the only way you teach "come." Remember that 90% of the time, your dog will need to come when there is something more interesting to look at.

The other way to train "come" is when he is distracted. This can be taught on a leash as well. To do any type of leash training to "come," you should do the following:

1. Place your dog on the leash. Either have him do a "sit"-"stay" or let him forage out ahead of you. I recommend using a 20 foot lead for this so you can introduce come at different distances.

2. If he is in a "sit"-"stay," walk away from the dog and then give the command for "come." If he is foraging ahead, wait until your

Tibetan Mastiff is distracted.

3. Give the command, "Come," and then encourage the dog to come to you by clapping your thighs, being excited and so on. Wave a treat out for him. Do not repeat the command.

4. If the dog doesn't come, start winding him in with the leash.

5. When the dog reaches you, either on his own or by being reeled in, use the treat to guide him into a "sit" without giving the command.

6. Praise the dog, touch his collar and treat.

7. Continue training "Come" over several weeks. After your puppy becomes adept at "Come" at a few feet, increase the distance slightly. The goal is to work up until your dog can be 100 or more feet from you and still "Come" when called, whether on the leash or off.

e. "Focus"

Not everyone teaches "focus" but it's useful because it is just a quick reminder to the dog that they need to focus on their handler. To teach "focus," all you need is a treat.

1. Have the dog sit or stand in front of you.

2. Place a treat in your hand and place it against his nose. Do not let him take it.

3. Raise the treat slowly to your face, near your eyes.

4. Give the command, "Focus" or "Watch."

5. When he glances in your eyes, praise and then give the treat.

6. Repeat until you don't need to bait him to focus with a treat.

f. "Drop It!"

"Drop it" can be a life saving command since it will get your Tibetan Mastiff to drop anything that you do not want them to have. "Drop it" is quite easy to teach but you need to set your dog up for the exercise or wait for him to have something that you need to take. To train "drop it," do the following:

1. Have the dog grab something with his mouth. Playing fetch is a great way to encourage this.

2. Once he has something in his mouth, grab it with one hand. In the other, have a treat.

3. Give the command, "Drop It."

4. Place the treat near his nose so he can smell it. He should drop the item.

5. If he does, praise and treat.

6. If he doesn't, you can place your hand over his nose. This will cause him to drop it as it is difficult to breath and uncomfortable for the dog.

7. When he drops the item, act like he did it without being forced; praise and treat.

g. "Leave It!"

"Leave it," like "drop it," is another command that could save your dog's life. Teaching them to leave things alone on the ground will keep them from eating dangerous items on walks. To teach "leave it," you want to work in stages. Start by leaving things in your hands and then moving up to leaving things on the ground.

1. Place a treat in your hand and close your fist.

2. Hold it in front of your dog and give the command, "Leave it."

3. Allow him to sniff the treat and try to get at it but ignore him when he is doing this.

4. Once he stops, even for a second, praise the dog and give him a treat with your other hand. Do not give the treat from the hand you told him to leave.

5. Repeat.

6. Increase the difficulty as your dog gets better with the command. Place the treat on your open hand, then on the ground under your cupped hand, and then on the ground without your hand covering. Always treat the dog when he visibly leaves the treat when you give the command.

h. Housetraining

The final section on training that I want to cover is housetraining. Although we focus on the dog learning to not go inside the house, it is more about training the owner to watch the puppy. The simple fact of housetraining is that a puppy needs to go to the bathroom every few hours, and accidents often happen because owners are not properly watching the dog.

For that reason, it is important to really follow the rules to housetraining. If you follow them, you will find your Tibetan Mastiff is housetrained very quickly.

Rule Number 1: Keep Watch on your Puppy
The first rule with housetraining is to watch your puppy. Generally, the puppy will give cues, such as sniffing around, going to squat, going to the door, and so on, that will indicate that your Tibetan Mastiff has to go to the bathroom.

If you are unable to watch your puppy, place him in a crate or somewhere secure where there is a non-porous flooring. Generally, puppies will not soil their bed so if you keep your Tibetan Mastiff in his bed when you can't watch him, you will be less likely to have an accident.

Rule Number 2: Understand When your Puppy has to Go
Another important rule is to understand when your puppy has to go to the bathroom. In general, puppies will have to go to the bathroom after the following:

- 5 to 20 minutes after eating or drinking
- When they first wake up
- After a play period
- Every 30 to 45 minutes when awake

By following this rule and taking your puppy out after each of these common times for them to go to the bathroom, you should be able to prevent 95% of the accidents that might occur.

Rule Number 3: Don't Scold
If you scold your puppy when you see him squatting or peeing you are likely to scare him into peeing again right away. Nothing positive is accomplished with scolding a puppy who pees in the house. The only thing you have accomplished is making your puppy afraid of you.

Instead, when an accident happens, clap your hands or say, "No" if the dog is in the middle of going to the bathroom. This will break the action and often puppies will stop urinating mid-stream.

As soon as he stops, scoop him up and take him outside immediately. Once he starts again, praise him.
When you are cleaning up the area, place the puppy in his crate and then clean it up where he can't see it.

When you clean up an accident, be sure you clean it up thoroughly. Puppies will always be tempted to return to places where they have pottied before.

Rule Number Four: Be Persistent
Although it may seem like you are outside all the time, it is important to be persistent. Take your Tibetan Mastiff outside and wait 10 to 15 minutes or until he has gone to the bathroom.

If he hasn't gone to the bathroom after the allotted time, pick him up and place him in his crate. Don't scold or tell him he is bad, simply place him in his crate. Wait about 5 to 10 minutes and then take him outside again.

Repeat the process until he has gone to the bathroom. The reason why you are placing him in his crate is to prevent him coming inside and immediately going to the bathroom.

Rule Number Five: Praise, Praise and Praise
Finally, make sure you praise your dog. You can wait til he squats outside and starts going to the bathroom, and then the entire time he is going say, "Good dog, go do your business." "Do your business" becomes a command for the dog. While your dog won't defecate on command, when you say, "Do your business," the dog will know that now isn't the time to sniff around and play and he will go to the bathroom.

For dogs that are harder to housetrain, you can treat the dog whenever he goes outside. This will quickly teach him that going to the bathroom outside is a very good thing.

And those are the basics of training your Tibetan Mastiff. Remember that training lasts the life of your dog and you should spend time every day working on different lessons, even when he is fully trained.

Chapter Eight: Feeding your Tibetan Mastiff

Although feeding your Tibetan Mastiff does not have to be any more complicated than simply pouring dog food into a bowl, it's best if owners understand dog food and feeding. Providing your dog with the best possible diet goes a long way in boosting his health.

In addition, avoiding foods with a lot of fillers and chemicals by buying high quality foods will help reduce the risk of some health problems.

Types of Food

When we are looking at feeding a Tibetan Mastiff, it is important to look at the various foods that you can offer your dog. There are hundreds of different dog food brands available so it can be a little overwhelming when you're trying to select one.

Many people like grain free dog foods today. Grain free foods have some benefits but they are misunderstood by many dog owners. You can also find good quality dog foods that contain some grains. As long as your dog does not have an allergy or food sensitivity to a particular grain, there is no reason to avoid it. Some dogs do have problems with corn, wheat, or soy, but dogs are more likely to be allergic to ingredients such as beef, chicken, lamb, fish, and even eggs and dairy. These are all common ingredients in dog food. In truth, only a small percentage of dogs has food allergies.

You can generally identify good quality foods by the following factors:

- Fewer grains (but not necessarily grain free)

- Lower carbs

- Two or three named meats in the first several ingredients

- Named fats

- No artificial preservatives, flavourings, sweeteners, or colours/dyes

- No ingredients with "digests;" better foods contain no meat by-products

- Human grade ingredients are preferred (though, legally, this is controversial since pet food cannot be sold as human food; but the ingredients should be fit for human consumption before they are made into pet food)

In the United States pet foods should have AAFCO approval (Association of American Feed Control Officials), indicating that they have passed minimum nutritional standards. In Europe, the EU Commission and other entities provide pet food regulations.

In general, most dogs do best on a diet that is high in protein and which has moderate fat. Giant breeds, and especially giant breed puppies, need to have food that is slightly lower in calories. Puppies need to grow slowly. Fast growth can lead to arthritis and other joint problems when the dog is older.

Whenever you change food, whether you are feeding a puppy or an adult dog, you need to do so slowly, over several days to avoid stomach upset. You will need to feed your puppy the food he has been used to eating at the breeder's home at first and then slowly make any changes to his diet.

There are actually four types of food that you can feed your dog. With dog food brands, it really is about doing research and finding the right dog food for you and your Tibetan Mastiff.

Food Type Number One: Dry Food

The most common and least expensive food that you can give your dog is dry food. This includes pellets, flaked food, mixes, biscuits, and kibbles. Kibble is very popular. It is easier to store and, per pound, if you are feeding a large dog, it is often the best choice.

Food Type Number Two: Wet Food

Wet food is food that usually comes in a can and has the consistency of canned fish. It has a very high moisture level and is usually higher in calories than dry food. It can be more expensive than dry food.

Wet food is not practical for most very large dogs because of the cost per ounce and the fact that you would have to feed your dog numerous cans per day. However, you can use it as a topping for your dog's kibble or a special meal. If you give it to your Tibetan Mastiff, remember to adjust the amount of kibble you are feeding. Otherwise your dog could develop a weight problem.

Food Type Number Three: Semi-moist Food

Semi-moist food comes in small pouch and usually has a kibble like shape in a meaty gravy. Like wet food, it is usually more expensive than dry. It is usually done as a treat for a dog since it is quite expensive.

Like wet, it works well when you blend it with dry food as a topping or treat.

Food Type Number Four: RAW/Homemade Food

The final type of food that you can give your dog is RAW food or a homemade diet. RAW has a lot of benefits including giving your dog high quality nutrients and a lot of variety. You can tailor the food to your individual Tibetan Mastiff's needs and you can change it slightly to add in fruits and vegetables.
In addition to the variety, dogs tend to use more of the RAW diet than they do with the dry kibble so it means less waste to be picked up.

The downside to RAW is that there can be some risk of salmonella and other bacterial poisoning if the food is not properly made or stored. In addition, if you are creating the recipes yourself, you could end up with nutritional deficiencies in your Tibetan Mastiff.

It is important to do the research before feeding any type of food. Make sure that it is complete, of a good quality, and free of chemicals. If you do that, your dog should be healthy.

Feeding your Tibetan Mastiff

Feeding your Tibetan Mastiff can be quite easy. It is important to note that how you feed, when you feed and how much you feed will be different depending on your dog and the food that you are using.

When to Feed

When to feed depends on the age of your dog and also on your schedule. With new Tibetan Mastiff puppy owners, you should feed your puppy three times per day: once in the morning, once around lunch time, and once in the evening.

As your puppy grows, you can begin to leave out the lunch feeding and move to two meals a day. Never feed only one meal a day. One meal can cause the dog to have some stomach problems and the dog may not eat as much in one sitting.

While your Tibetan Mastiff is eating breakfast, get ready for your day and then he will be ready to go outside right before you leave for work.

In the evening, feed when you get home from work, or around dinner time, and he will have gone outside before bedtime. And that is really all there is to the time to feed your dog.

How much to Feed

Feeding differs depending on the age of your dog, how active the dog is and the type of food you are feeding. High quality dog foods require less food while low quality foods require more, so your dog can reach the necessary caloric intake. With feeding, it is important to look at the weight of your dog, as well as his energy level and age.

To do this, we have to look at the resting energy requirements. What this means is that when your dog is resting, how many calories is the dog burning? From there, we can begin to adjust the amount of food, or calories that we need to feed the dog.

Determining your dog's resting energy requirements is simple. Take your dog's weight in kilograms and multiply it by 30. Then add 70. So if you have a 23 pound Tibetan Mastiff, you would divide 23 by 2.2 for a total of 10.45 or 10.5 if we round up. Multiply 10.5 by 30 for 315 and then add 70 for a total of 385 calories per day. Most dog food bags have the calorie amount for every half cup or cup so you simply divide the calories needed by the calories provided.

For instance, Purina Dog Chow Complete Nutrition has 430 calories for every cup of dog food. So dividing 430 into 385 means that the dog would need slightly more than 3/4 cups of food to meet his caloric intake needs. This is the resting energy requirement for a dog. But dogs have all kinds of situations. A dog might be pregnant or neutered or have light activity, for example. You can check the chart below to find the number to muliply by your dog's resting energy requirement.

Activity Level/Age	Multiplier for Resting Energy Requirements
Weaning to 4 months	X 3.0
4 months to adult	X 2.0
Lactating female	X 4.8
Pregnant female day 1 to 42	X 1.8
Pregnant female day 42 to whelping	X 3.0
Adult Dog neutered/spayed with normal activity	X 1.6
Adult Dog intact with normal activity	X 1.8

Adult Dog with light activity X 2.0
Adult Dog with moderate activity   X 3.0
Adult Dog with heavy activity   X 4.8
Adult Dog with weight loss X 1.0

As you can see, the daily calories can change depending on the individual dog. So if the same Tibetan Mastiff from above, who needs 385 calories per day, was a lactating female that was nursing puppies, her calories for the day should be 1848 or 4 and a quarter cups of Purina Dog Chow.

Fortunately, most dog food companies have already done this math for you. The guidelines that they include on their labels are based on these figures so you can use their suggestions for how much to feed your dog as a starting point. You will need to watch your puppy or dog when you start feeding him a dog food to see if he is gaining or losing weight and his overall condition. You can make adjustments to his portions accordingly.

When we are looking at RAW feeding, the amounts are slightly different. In addition, it is difficult to determine the calories as it will be different with the feed you are giving. A pound of beef with 30% blend of organ, meat and bone has about 2600 calories in it, so the Tibetan Mastiff that weighs 23 pounds only needs about 0.2 pounds of food per day. The reason for this is because the multiplier for the resting energy requirements is higher when feeding raw, which is outlined in the chart below.

Activity Level/Age	Multiplier for Resting Energy Requirements
Weaning to 4 months	X 6.0
4 months to adult	X 4.0
Lactating female	X 8.0
Pregnant female day 1 to 42	X 4.0
Pregnant female day 42 to whelping	X 6.0
Adult Dog neutered/spayed with normal activity	X 2.0
Adult Dog intact with normal activity	X 2.5
Adult Dog with light activity	X 3.0
Adult Dog with moderate activity	X 3.5
Adult Dog with heavy activity	X 4.0
Adult Dog with weight loss	X 1.5

How to Feed

When we talk about how to feed, it isn't just putting the food into a bowl. Instead, what we are talking about is whether to free feed or not. If you are not sure what free feeding is, it is when you place the dog's food in a dish and allow him access to it constantly.

While this may seem like a great idea, and your dog may like it, it's not advisable. Free feeding can lead to many problems such as aggression, obesity and even weight loss if you have other pets in the home who are eating all the food.

Instead of free feeding, make set mealtimes for feeding. Pour the desired amount into the bowl and then give the dog 20 minutes to finish it. If the dog hasn't finished his meal, pick it up and save the food for his next meal time.

If your dog doesn't eat his meals at first, he will eventually (unless something is medically wrong). Feeding in this manner will allow you to keep track of his calorie intake and also prevent food bowl aggression.

Watering your Tibetan Mastiff

A Tibetan Mastiff should be offered water throughout the day and it should be adjusted according to the season. They will drink more water during the hot summer months than during the winter. Water should be cool but be careful with ice cold water. Too much ice cold water and it can lead to digestive problems with your Tibetan Mastiff.

Young puppies that are not fully housetrained should only be offered water at set times. This will help reduce the number of times the puppy has to go to the bathroom. Another rule with young dogs is to pick up the water dish about 2 hours before you go to bed. This will help your puppy make it through the night without an accident.

With adult dogs, or housetrained dogs, you can leave the water down all the time.

To determine if your dog has enough water in the day, you should follow the rule of weight. In general, you should give your dog 1 ounce of water for every pound he weighs, or 66ml for every kilogram of dog.

Treats for your Tibetan Mastiff

Walk through a pet store and you will see that there are hundreds of different treats for your Tibetan Mastiff. Really, getting a treat for your dog is as simple as walking into a store. But there are a few things to consider before buying treats.

The first thing is that treats are just that -- treats. You should never just feed the treats without thinking about the added calories. Yes, even Tibetan Mastiff need to watch their waistline and feeding treats freely can lead to obesity in your dog. It's estimated that over 50 percent of all dogs are overweight or obese.

A general rule of thumb to follow with treats is to only allow them to take up 10% of your dog's daily calories. In addition, always include the calories as part of your dog's daily caloric intake.

When you are selecting treats for your dogs, follow these rules:

Tip Number One: Avoid Table Scraps
While it can be tempting to feed your dog from the table, you should avoid it. The main reason is that a lot of human food contains additives that can be harmful to your Tibetan Mastiff. Read the next section on foods to avoid for more information.

Tip Number Two: Choose Natural Ingredients
When you are purchasing treats from the store, read the ingredient label. Only choose foods that have natural ingredients and avoid foods with processed ingredients.

Tip Number Three: Don't Buy Products Made in China
Although most of the products are safe for your dog, it is

important to remember that products made in China do not have all the safety restrictions that they do in other countries. Many products are made with serious chemicals that have been linked to liver disease, cancer and that have even resulted in death.

Tip Number Four: Try to Use Fresh Foods
While we often think of dog treats as bones or manufactured foods, they can be as simple as giving your dog a carrot. In fact, many fruits and vegetables are safe for your Tibetan Mastiff and make an excellent treat for your dog.

Tip Number Five: Think of Health Benefits
Finally, when you are choosing your treats, think of health options. Many treats have supplements in them that will help prevent arthritis, boost your dog's immune system and a range of other benefits so check the ingredient list for healthy vitamins and to make sure there are no chemicals in the food.

Here's a list of healthy snack choices for your Tibetan Mastiff:

Apples: remove seeds	Kale
Applesauce	Lemons
Apricots: remove pits	Marrow Bones
Baby food: all-natural, make sure it is free of salt	Mint
Bananas	Nectarines: remove pits
Beef: raw and cooked	Oatmeal
Beets	Organ meats: heart, liver, kidney, etc.
Blackberries	Pasta: cooked
Blueberries	Peaches: remove pits
Bran cereal	Peanut butter
Bread: avoid nut breads	Pears

and raison bread
Broccoli: safe when fed raw
Brussels Sprouts
Cantaloupe
Carrots
Cauliflower: safe when fed raw

Celery
Cheerio's
Cheese: cheddar is safe
Chicken: remove bones if cooked
Corn: safe off the cob
Cottage cheese
Cranberries
Cream cheese
Cucumbers
Dog Cookies: homemade and store bought
Eggs: when cooked
Green beans

Honey

Peas
Pineapple
Plums: remove pits
Pumpkin
Rice: cooked only

Rice cakes
Salmon
Spinach
Squash

Strawberries
Sweet potatoes
Tomatoes
Training treats
Tuna
Turkey: cooked with bones removed
Watermelon
Yogurt

Foods to Avoid

Here are some foods that you should never feed your dog. While some foods are safe for people, there are a range of foods that can have catastrophic effects on your Tibetan Mastiff if you feed them to him.

Below is a chart that goes over foods you should avoid giving to your dog.

Foods to Avoid	Reasons to Avoid
Alcohol	Can lead to a coma and/or death
Apple Seeds	Seeds contain cyanide and can lead to death.
Artificial Sweetener	Can cause low blood sugar, vomiting, collapse and liver failure.
Avocado	May cause vomiting and diarrhea
Broccoli	When cooked, it can cause gas, which can lead to bloat. Safe when it is raw.
Cat Food	While not harmful, too much cat food can lead to health problems due to the high protein and fat content.
Cauliflower	When cooked, it can cause gas, which can lead to bloat. Safe when it is raw.
Chocolate	Contains caffeine and theobromine and can lead to vomiting and diarrhea. Can lead to death if too much is consumed.
Chicken	Cooked chicken has bones that will splinter, which can

	lead to an obstruction or laceration in the digestive system.
Citrus	May cause vomiting.
Citrus Oil	May cause vomiting.
Coffee	Contains caffeine and can lead to vomiting and diarrhea. Can lead to death if too much is consumed.
Currants	Can cause kidney damage and death.
Fat Trimmings	High fat levels can lead to pancreatitis.
Fish	Bones can lacerate the digestive system. In addition, if fed a fish exclusive diet, it can lead to vitamin B deficiency, which can cause seizures and death. Fish in dog food is fine as long as other nutrients are in the ingredients list.
Garlic	Can cause anaemia.
Grapes	Can cause kidney damage and death.
Grape Seed Oil	Can cause kidney damage and death.
Gum	Can cause blockages but contains Xylitol, which can damage the liver.
Hops	Can cause increased heart

	rate, fever, seizures and sometimes, death.
Human Vitamins	Can damage a dog's liver, kidneys and digestive system.
Macadamia Nuts	Toxin in the nuts can cause seizures and death.
Milk	Along with other dairy products, can cause diarrhea.
Mushrooms	Can cause shock, shut down multiple body systems and can lead to death.
Onions	Can cause anaemia.
Persimmons	The seeds lead to intestinal obstructions.
Peaches	The flesh of the peach is fine, however, be sure to remove the pit or it can cause an obstruction.
Pork	Has bones that will splinter, which can lead to an obstruction or laceration in the digestive system.
Plums	The flesh of the plum is fine, however, be sure to remove the pit or it can cause an obstruction.
Raisins	Can cause kidney damage and death.

Rhubarb Leaves	Poisonous, can affect the urinary tract system, digestive system and nervous system.
Salt	Can lead to vomiting, diarrhea, dehydration and seizures. Large quantities can lead to death.
Sugar	Leads to obesity and has been linked to canine diabetes.
Tea	Contains caffeine and can lead to vomiting and diarrhea. Can lead to death if too much is consumed.
Tomato Greens/Plant	Can cause heart problems in dogs.
Turkey	Cooked turkey has bones that will splinter, which can lead to an obstruction or laceration in the digestive system.
Yeast	Can cause pain, gas and can even cause a rupture in the digestive system, which can result in death.

Chapter Nine: Socializing and Training your Tibetan Mastiff

One important aspect of owning a Tibetan Mastiff is to properly train and socialize your puppy and your dog. While many people think of socializing and training as something you do when your Tibetan Mastiff is a puppy, it is actually important to do both throughout the life of your dog.

Even a perfectly trained dog will slip into some bad habits. If you spend just a few minutes a day on training, you can keep this from happening.

In this chapter we'll go over the key points of socializing and training your Tibetan Mastiff. This chapter in no way replaces the advice and training of a professional dog trainer. We strongly suggest you enroll your Tibetan Mastiff puppy in puppy kindergarten or puppy preschool classes. And we encourage you to follow up with a good basic obedience class when your puppy is a little older.

Socializing your Tibetan Mastiff

Socializing your Tibetan Mastiff is an important step in developing a well rounded dog. In many ways, socialization begins the moment the puppies are born. There are many things that your breeder will do that will establish good socialization patterns with the puppies.

Generally, when we think of socialization, we think of it in terms of being social with others. This can be with people, other dogs, or children. While being "social" is one important aspect of socializing, it is just that, one aspect.

Instead of focusing socialization on one area, it's important to focus on socializing the complete dog. Socialize the dog to a range of stimuli and this will help create a sound dog that doesn't frighten easily. The whole point of socialization is to build self-confidence in your dog so he can calmly interact with the human world. Let's look at ways to build that confidence.

What is Socialization?

Socialization means to be part of society. What this means when we apply it to dogs is that a dog needs to be a productive part of their human surroundings. They should be taught to accept things they will see on a day to day basis. In addition, they should accept people and other animals.

Socialization is when we expose a puppy and/or dog to a host of different stimuli and encourage them to accept or not even notice that stimuli.

The process of socialization is very important since dogs who are not properly socialized can become timid and fearful. In addition, they can become aggressive to animals, other dogs, and to people.

When Should I Socialize?

Socialization is a lifelong process, however, socialization should begin as soon as a puppy comes home. Socialization outside the home should start at around 12 weeks old when a puppy has been properly vaccinated.

The key period of socialization is between the ages of 12 weeks to

5 months old. During that time, your Tibetan Mastiff will go through various developmental milestones, which will go smoothly if socialization is done properly.

In addition to these periods, you should be aware that puppies will go through fear periods. Your confident Tibetan Mastiff may suddenly become a very fearful little puppy almost overnight. This is normal and you simply continue socializing your puppy as you normally would.

Fear periods in dogs differ depending on the breed but you should expect it to be between 5 to 7 months old and then, possibly, again around 16 to 18 months of age.

How do I socialize?

Socialization is done in small amounts and it is important to follow a few rules to help keep socialization positive. Remember that you want your Tibetan Mastiff to accept things as a positive and not to be afraid. If something is negative, then the dog will have more problems than if he wasn't socialized at all.

Rule Number One: Make the Socialization Fun
Always make sure that every socialization time that he has is a fun one. Let the puppy play around the stimuli so that he can learn that it is not a negative thing.

Rule Number Two: Let It Be at His Pace
Although our first response is to nudge our puppy closer to the thing we are socializing him to, it is important to allow your Tibetan Mastiff to approach the object at his own pace.

It may take several socialization experiences before the puppy will go and approach the new item but you should take your time.

Never force the experience or push the dog towards the stimuli.

Rule Number Three: Give your Tibetan Mastiff Space
Sit close to your Tibetan Mastiff so you can be a reassurance to him but also let him have space. You want him to feel like he can retreat and approach the stimuli as he likes. If he feels cornered or trapped, it will make the socialization a negative experience.

When it comes to people, use the same rule. Have them sit away from the puppy and then allow the puppy to go and greet them.

Rule Number Four: Mix it Up
Another important rule is to mix up the socialization. Your Tibetan Mastiff may have no problem interacting with dogs when he is in his home but outside of his home may be a different story. Take the time to set up socialization outside of the house and in the house. Take him to lots of places, introduce him to the same things you introduced in the home, within reason -- for instance, you are not as likely to run into a vacuum on the street.

Do the reverse when he is at home. Often, people forget the importance of inviting others over so the Tibetan Mastiff can learn to accept things both in his house and outside of it. Remember, the Tibetan Mastiff can be very territorial so you want to make visitors an accepted norm.

Rule Number Five: Use Reinforcement
Finally, use rewards for reinforcement when you are socializing your puppy. Things like treats, verbal encouragement, and praise will help your Tibetan Mastiff be successful with a socialization exercise.

One word of caution with rewards is to never reward your dog when he is scared. This includes babying the dog when he is frightened or giving a negative reinforcement when he doesn't socialize the way you want him to.

Babying will only let your puppy know that it is okay to be scared and correction or negative reinforcement will make the Tibetan Mastiff more fearful than he already is. So, no coddling. You want to encourage your puppy to be brave.

What Should I Socialize To?

You may be wondering what you should use for socializing your puppy. While everyone has different living circumstances that will change your socialization stimuli, there are a number of stimuli that you should use for your puppy no matter where you live. Below is a checklist to get you started with socializing your Tibetan Mastiff.

Stimuli	X	Stimuli	X
Men: Bearded and not		Balls of various size	
Women		Mirrors	
Children: Boys and Girls		Baby strollers	
Toddlers: Boys and Girls		Grocery carts	
Babies: Boys and Girls		Mirrors	
People with glasses		Brooms	
People with crutches		Dusters	
People with canes		Vacuum cleaners	
People in wheelchairs		Wind	
Slouched people		Flags	
People with walkers		Tents	
Shuffling people		Flashlights	
Large crowds		Kid Toys	
Small crowds		Television	

People on roller blades	Plastic bags
People of various shapes and sizes: tall, thin, heavy, short, etc.	Umbrellas
People with sunglasses	Balloons
People who are exercising	Skateboards
People on bikes	Children playing
Costumes	Hammering
Bald people	Construction equipment
Big dogs	Lawn mowers
Little dogs	Scooters
Farm Animals	Buses
Puppies	Trains
Small Rodent/non canine	Sirens
Birds	Ceiling fans
Lizards	Garage doors
Escalators	Dremel tools
Cars: Both walking and riding in	Fireworks
Sliding doors	Cheering
Planes (optional)	Yelling
Elevators	Radios
Escalators	Storms
Alarms	Loud noises
Singing	Visiting the vet
Grooming	Getting nails cut
Being crated	Being picked up
Having all body parts touched	Leash

Collar   Harnesses

As you can see, there is a lot to socialize your Tibetan Mastiff to and these only touch on some of the more common stimuli.

Training your Tibetan Mastiff

This section will cover training your Tibetan Mastiff. We want to say, again, that puppy classes and working with a professional trainer are highly recommended. While a lot of training can be done at home, puppy kindergarten and obedience training will help prevent mistakes and will offer ample socialization to your puppy.

Tibetan Mastiffs are intelligent but headstrong. They are trainable but, unlike many working breeds, they do not respond to training as quickly as many owners might wish. Before you start training your puppy or dog, make up your mind that this process might take some time. You should adjust your expectations and be happy with small degrees of progress. They are smart dogs and they can learn quickly. Whether they choose to obey you is another matter.

That said, do not imagine for one moment that you can bully this breed into compliance. As said earlier, Tibetan Mastiffs expect to be companions and partners. However, it is important for you to be calmly in charge. You can't train your dog if you are confused about whether you or your dog is in command.

The Tibetan Mastiff does require rules and it is important to be consistent with them. Before you bring your puppy home, think of the rules that you want to have in your house. If you are fine with dogs on the furniture, allow it. If not, don't allow it from the very moment your puppy comes home. It may not seem like a big deal but it will confuse your Tibetan Mastiff when you finally tell him to stay off.

When you are training your Tibetan Mastiff, be sure to follow these rules:

Rule Number One: Be First
When it comes to establishing yourself as the leader in your home, make sure that you are always the first. Go through doors before your Tibetan Mastiff, eat first, go downstairs first and so on.

Rule Number Two: Make him Work
Regardless of whether you are giving him food, a treat or praise, you want your dog to work for it. Always give your Tibetan Mastiff a command, such as "sit" and "wait" at dinner time, before you give him some form of reward. This will teach him that he needs to work for things and will also help with manners so he is not jumping or grabbing at things.

Rule Number Three: Be the Initiator
Playing, cuddling, and any type of attention should be done with you initiating it. Pick up toys, although you can leave out a few to combat chewing, and bring them out for play sessions.
Do not give in if he brings the toys to you and is pushy to get you to play. In addition, don't pay attention to your Tibetan Mastiff if he is jumping or biting at you to get attention. Instead, ignore him until he is sitting politely and then give him the attention. Again, this goes back to working for things since sitting nicely is working.

Rule Number Four: Give your Tibetan Mastiff his own Space
While it can be tempting to keep your dog with you at all times, make sure that you give him his own space as well. Crate training

is recommended since it keeps puppies from chewing when you aren't home. You can also give your dog his own bed area.

This area will give him a chance to take a break when the house is too busy or he is tired. In addition, it will be a safe place for him and that will help in establishing roles in your home. Not only will he feel secure with you in charge, but also with his role in the house.

Note that Tibetan Mastiff puppies can be terrible chewers. They are quite happy to cut their teeth on your woodwork or dining room table. The more toys you provide for them, the better. Providing some toys in their crate when you can't watch them is often a good idea.

Rule Number Five: Always have Access to his Food
Finally, always make sure that you have access to your dog's food dish. When he is a puppy, take the time to have your hands in his dish and also make sure that you feed him a few handfuls.

If your Tibetan Mastiff becomes too pushy when you are in the dish, lift it up and only feed him by hand until he relaxes. You want to make it clear that the food dish belongs to you and he is simply allowed to eat from it.

You also want to teach him that the food will be given back to him when he behaves. Have everyone in the house do the food dish exercise. While it will help with establishing leadership, it also helps with preventing food guarding or aggression.

Tibetan Mastiffs often tend to have issues about food. They can guard their food, dump their food, try to gulp it all down at one go, and show other extraordinary behaviours. You may have to work on your puppy's food issues from a young age to help him relax about them.

In the end, when you are training your Tibetan Mastiff, it comes down to being consistent, firm and making it fun. If you do that, along with providing strong leadership, you will make progress with training your Tibetan Mastiff.

Chapter Ten: Tibetan Mastiff Health

Tibetan Mastiff are considered to be a healthy breed with very few health problems. That being said, there are a number of diseases that affect the Tibetan Mastiff and it is important to make sure that you purchase a dog from a reputable breeder.

Generally, a reputable breeder will have parents health tested before they breed them. The tests that are important with the Tibetan Mastiff are:

- Eyes Certified by a board-certified ACVO Ophthalmologist

- OFA or PennHip certification for Hip Dysplasia
- OFA evaluation for Autoimmune Thyroiditis

- OFA evaluation for elbow dysplasia is optional in the breed.

By purchasing from a breeder who health tests his or her lines, you are less likely to run into the hereditary illnesses that can affect the breed.

However, even with the best screening, some diseases can get still occur. This chapter is about identifying illnesses in your dog as well as common health problems you may see in your Tibetan Mastiff.

Signs of Illness

Although signs of illness may differ depending on the disease or illness affecting a dog, there are some general signs that you should look out for. When your Tibetan Mastiff has any of these symptoms, it is important to seek veterinarian care.

One thing that must be stressed with any breed, including the Tibetan Mastiff, is that often illnesses are sudden and it is very easy for a dog to go from healthy to gravely ill. Make sure you monitor your dog frequently and do a daily health check on your Tibetan Mastiff.

Symptoms that your dog may be sick are:

Bad Breath

Bad breath is often a sign of some oral problem but it can also be a sign of other diseases. If your dog has bad breath, and there is no root cause for it that you can see, schedule an appointment with your vet.

Drooling

Tibetan Mastiff can drool at times but excess drooling is a tip off that there could be a health problem. If your dog is drooling a lot, make an appointment to see your vet right away.

Loss of Appetite

Loss of appetite is often one of the first indicators that something is wrong with your Tibetan Mastiff. With loss of appetite, it is very important to look at the pattern of eating. If your dog is usually a picky eater, missing the occasional meal should not give rise to concerns.

In addition, if you have a female that has not been spayed, she may stop eating around her heat cycles. Pregnancy can also lead to a dog not eating as much.

The biggest concern is when your dog is not eating for more than 24 hours, especially if other symptoms are seen.

Excessive Thirst

Outside of days with hot weather, if your Tibetan Mastiff seems to be drinking large amounts of water, then it could be an indication of disease or dehydration. In general, a Tibetan Mastiff should drink about an ounce of water for every pound of dog.

Changes in Urination

Changes in the colour of urine as well as the frequency of urination can indicate a health problem. It is important to note that an increase in urination can be linked to some illnesses while difficulty urinating can indicate other problems.

If you spot blood in the urine, contact your vet immediately.

Skin Problems

If your dog's skin is a bright red or you see flaking skin, then it could be a problem with your dog's health.

In addition, if the dog is itching a lot, you could have fleas, some type of mite, or the dog could also have allergies. Make sure you check off all the reasons for the skin problems.

Lethargy

Tibetan Mastiffs may like to sleep during the day but they should not be lethargic. Like changes in appetite, make sure that you identify any reasons why your dog is tired, such as being over-exercised. If there are no apparent reasons, contact your vet.

Gum Problems

Although we see gum problems as being linked to teeth or gum disease, they can actually be linked to other serious diseases that can affect your Tibetan Mastiff. Things to look for are:

☐ *Swollen Gums:* Swollen gums, when accompanied by bad breath, can indicate gum disease or other oral problems.

☐ *Bright Red Gums:* When a dog's gums are bright red, it could be an indication that the dog is fighting an infection. Exposures to toxins is another reason for bright red gums. Or your dog could have heatstroke.

☐ *Blue Gums:* With blue gums, what you are seeing is that the Tibetan Mastiff is lacking oxygen for some reason. Seek immediate veterinarian care.

☐ *Purple Gums:* Purple gums are often seen when a dog has gone into shock or there is a problem with his blood circulation. What has happened before you notice the purple gums in your Tibetan Mastiff will indicate whether the dog is in shock or not.

☐ *Grey Gums:* The same as purple gums, when grey gums are

seen in a Tibetan Mastiff, it can indicate either poor blood circulation or shock.

☐ *Pale Pink:* Pale pink gums can be an indication of anaemia in the Tibetan Mastiff.

☐ *White Gums:* Finally, white gums can be an indication of a loss of blood. This loss can be either externally or internally so contact your vet immediately.

As you can see, gums are one of the primary indicators of illness in dogs. If your dog does not have pink gums, but has black instead, you can check his health by looking at the pink portion of his lower eyelid.

Changes in Weight

This is something that is not always easy to follow since it means relying on charting his weight, but if you notice unexpected weight loss or weight gain in your Tibetan Mastiff, there could be an underlying condition.

Stiffness of Limbs

Tibetan Mastiffs are not usually stiff in their limbs. While old age can create some stiffness, there are several diseases that can affect mobility. If you notice difficulty in getting up, climbing stairs or walking, there may be an underlying problem.

Respiratory Problems

Whenever you see excessive sneezing, coughing, laboured breathing and panting, take note. It could be nothing, but often respiratory problems are an early indication that there is a health problem.

Runny Eyes or Nose

If you see any discharge or fluid coming out of your Tibetan Mastiff's eyes or nose, keep close watch on his symptoms. This can be linked to several conditions including respiratory illnesses.

Vomiting and Gagging

Dog's will gag and vomit without being ill, however, if you see repeated vomiting or the dog has a bowed look and is continually gagging, seek medical help. Vomiting and gagging can be a sign of allergies or could indicate a life-threatening disease.

Fluctuations in Temperature

Finally, if you suspect that your Tibetan Mastiff's health is compromised, it is important to check your dog's temperature. Temperatures that are too high can indicate a fever, which could be a symptom of a serious disease. Too low could indicate other problems such as shock.

Check the temperature with a rectal thermometer or an ear thermometer. Make sure that the Tibetan Mastiff's temperature is between the following:

☐ *Rectal Temperature:* Rectal temperatures in dogs should be between 100.5 to 102.5°F (38 to 39.2°F)

☐ *Ear Temperature:* Ear temperatures in dogs should be between 100 to 103°F (37.7 to 39.4°C).

If you see a temperature of lower or higher, seek veterinarian help. One exception to the rule of temperatures is in pregnant females, read the chapter on breeding your Tibetan Mastiff for more information on this.

It is important to note that some symptoms, occurring on their own, may not indicate any problem. However, if your Tibetan Mastiff has three or more of the symptoms, you should seek medical care for your dog.

Common Health Problems in the Breed

Tibetan Mastiffs are, in general, a hardy breed. They have a life expectancy of 10 to 14 years. This is much longer than many breeds of comparable size. They tend to have fewer genetic health problems than some other breeds. However, there are between 400 and 500 genetic diseases known in domestic dogs and a few of them do exist in the Tibetan Mastiff.

a) Hypothyroidism

Hypothyroidism occurs when the thyroid is producing a lower amount of the hormones T4 and T3. It is a condition that is more commonly seen in dogs that have been altered as opposed to dogs that are intact.

This condition can be caused by other diseases and conditions or it can be hereditary. While it can affect a dog at any age, it is more commonly seen in dogs between the ages of 4 and 10 years old. It is relatively common in Tibetan Mastiffs, though normal values for the breed may be naturally lower than some other breeds.

Symptoms
There are many symptoms when a dog has a hypothyroid. These symptoms are:

- Weakness
- Mental dullness
- Seizures
- Hair loss and/or poor hair growth
- Dull coat
- Inactivity
- Lethargy
- Scaling on the skin
- Skin infections that reoccur
- Infertility
- Intolerance to cold

Treatment
Treatment is usually by inexpensive medication as well as exercise and a low fat diet. In addition to medication, synthetic hormones may be recommended for your dog.

b) entropion

Entropion is a genetic condition in which a portion of the eyelid is inverted or folded inward. This can cause an eyelash or hair to irritate and scratch the surface of the eye, leading to corneal ulceration or perforation. Entropion is fairly common in dogs and is seen in a wide variety of breeds, including short-nosed breeds, giant breeds, and sporting breeds. Entropion is almost always diagnosed around the time a puppy reaches its first birthday.

Symptoms
In toy and brachycephalic (short-nosed) breeds of dogs, excess

tears and/or inner eye inflammation are common signs of entropion. However, in giant breeds, it is more common to see mucus and/or pus discharge from the outer corner of the eyes. In other breeds of dogs, eye tics, discharge of pus, eye inflammation, or even rupture of the cornea are the typical signs of entropion.

Treatment
Underlying irritants should be removed before any attempt is made to correct the problem surgically. In some cases antibiotics or artificial tears can help with the problem but surgery is often required.

c) ectropion

Ectropion is a condition in which the margin of the lower eyelid rolls forward, exposing the haw, or pink part of the eye. Some of the giant breeds are more inclined to this problem, along with a few other breeds. It can occur in dogs less than one year old. It can come and go in some dogs, occurring when they are tired.

Symptoms

- Protrusion of the lower eyelid, and exposure of the inner lid
- Facial staining caused by poor tear drainage
- History of discharge from conjunctival exposure
- Recurrent foreign object irritation
- History of bacterial conjunctivitis

Treatment

A topical lubricant or antibiotic ointment, along with good eye and facial hygiene usually helps most dogs. Surgical treatment may be necessary in some cases.

d) distichiasis

Distichiasis is an eyelash disorder that is found in dogs. Distichiasis is an eyelash that grows from an abnormal spot on the eyelid. The eyelash hair can come into contact with and damage the cornea or conjunctiva of the eye. It is most commonly seen in young dogs. It is not considered common in Tibetan Mastiffs.

Symptoms

- Few, if any, symptoms can be seen
- Stiff eyelash
- Pawing at eye
- Abnormal tick or twitch of eyelid
- Overflow of tears
- Increased blood vessels in the cornea
- Change in iris pigmentation
- Corneal ulcers

Treatment

Removing the cause of irritation usually solves the problem. No treatment is usually necessary. Continue to remove the eyelash that grows out and bothers the eye. If the hair is a frequent irritation to the eye, surgery may be required.

e) demodex

Some Tibetan Mastiffs can get demodex or demodectic mange. Demodex is caused by tiny mites that feed on the hair follicles and glands of the skin. Demodex is considered to be less severe than sarcoptic mange. It is usually self-limiting. Once the mites are gone, the dog's immune system is usually able to keep them from returning. Some dogs, however, do not develop this immunity against the mites.

Symptoms
Demodectic mange may either be localized and affect specific areas of the body, or generalized, where it affects the entire body. If localized, symptoms are usually mild, with lesions occurring in patches, especially on the face, body, or legs. If generalized, symptoms will be more widespread and appear across the body. These symptoms include hair loss, a redness of the skin, and the appearance of scales and lesions.

Treatment
Localized demodex usually resolves itself. This happens in most cases. Generalized demodex, which is more severe, usually requires medication from your veterinarian.

f) Addison's Disease

Addison's Disease is relatively rare in dogs but it can occur in Tibetan Mastiffs. The adrenal gland produces certain hormones that are necessary in the body. With Addison's Disease, or Hypoadrenocorticism, the adrenal gland does not make enough mineralocorticoids and glucocorticoids that the body needs.

Symptoms

- Lethargy
- Lack of appetite
- Vomiting
- Weight loss
- Diarrhea
- Shaking
- Increased frequency of urination
- Increased thirst
- Depression
- Dehydration
- Weak pulse
- Collapse
- Low temperature
- Blood in feces
- Hair loss
- Painful abdomen

Treatment

An acute episode of Addison's Disease is a veterinary emergency and will require immediate hospitalization for treatment. Treatment depends on the dog and severity of symptoms. IV fluids may be necessary and it is usually necessary to replace deficient hormones. Hormone injections are standard for dogs that have been diagnosed.

g) Cushing's Disease

Cushing's Disease refers to Hyperadrenocorticism in dogs. It is a common endocrine disorder in dogs. When a disorder causes an excess of cortisone levels in the bloodstream, the metabolic process is hampered. This leads to gastrointestinal disorders and hypertension, among other bodily problems. Cushing's refers to cases that occur due to a benign pituitary gland tumour.

Symptoms

Increased thirst and urination (polydipsia and polyuria, respectively)

- Increased hunger
- Increased panting
- Pot-bellied abdomen
- Obesity
- Fat pads on the neck and shoulders
- Loss of hair
- Lack of energy
- Insomnia
- Muscle weakness
- Lack of a menstrual period
- Shrinking of testicles

- Darkening of the skin
- Appearance of blackheads on the skin
- Thin skin (from weight gain)
- Bruising (from thin, weakened skin)

Treatment
Many dogs can be treated with drugs but the drugs can have side effects. Whether drugs can be used or not depends on the type of tumour and its location. Small, non-spreading tumours and small cancerous tumours can be surgically removed.

h) epilepsy

Tibetan Mastiffs can have seizures. Some are epileptic in nature and others are not. Epilepsy can be genetic or it can occur for unknown (idiopathic) reasons. It is a brain disorder.

Symptoms
Seizures usually have a short aura before they begin. At this time the dog may seem frightened and confused. Some dogs hide or seek comfort. When the seizure starts, the dog will fall on his side, become stiff, chomp his jaws, salivate, urinate, defecate, vocalize, and may paddle with his limbs. These actions usually continue for between 30 and 90 seconds.

Seizures usually occur when the dog is resting or asleep, so they often happen at night or early in the morning. Most dogs have already recovered by the time the owner brings them to the vet.

If your dog has a seizure, you should stay back. Your dog is not aware of you and you could be accidentally bitten.

After the seizure, your dog may be confused. He may wander or pace. He may be very thirsty. Some dogs recover right away but it can take up to 24 hours for a dog to return to normal. Large breed dogs are more likely to have cluster seizures. This is especially true if they have a pattern of epilepsy.

Treatment
Dogs who start having seizures before they are two years old have a good chance of controlling their seizures with medication.

Dogs can take anti-epileptic and anti-convulsant medications. One of the side effects is a tendency to become overweight. Your dog may need a diet plan to help him with his weight.

i) progressive retinal atrophy (PRA)

Progressive retinal atrophy affects the retinas of a dog's eyes. When a dog has PRA, his photoreceptors deteriorate over time and eventually he becomes blind.

Symptoms
- Night blindness that progresses to blindness in light as well
- Dilated pupils
- Inability to see clearly in bright light
- In some conditions, only central vision may be lost, the animal may still retain peripheral vision
- The pupil has abnormal reactions to light
- The retinal structure appears abnormal when a doctor examines it with an ophthalmoscope; cataract may be observed
- The liver may also be affected, obesity may be observed

- Sudden blindness may be due to sudden acquired retinal degeneration syndrome (SARDS)

There are different kinds of PRA and it's actually a group of diseases. PRA can manifest differently in different breeds of dogs.

Treatment

There is no cure for PRA. Surgery does not help if your dog is blind and not in any pain. There are no current medications that can reverse this disease. However, diet can cause retinal degeneration. It is thought that a balanced, low fat diet can improve your dog's eyes.

j) hip or elbow dysplasia

The dog's hip joint is made up of a ball and socket. Genetics and the environment help determine how the joint fits together. If the joint does not fit right or if it begins to deteriorate, the dog can develop hip dysplasia. Hip dysplasia is one of the most common health problems seen in dogs.

Elbow dysplasia can refer to several physical problems that cause lameness, pain, or deterioration of the elbow joints.

Symptoms

Hip dysplasia
- Early disease: signs are related to joint looseness or laxity

- Later disease: signs are related to joint degeneration and osteoarthritis
- Decreased activity
- Difficulty rising
- Reluctance to run, jump, or climb stairs
- Intermittent or persistent hind-limb lameness, often worse after exercise
- "Bunny-hopping," or swaying gait
- Narrow stance in the hind limbs (back legs unnaturally close together)
- Pain in hip joints
- Joint looseness or laxity – characteristic of early disease; may not be seen in long-term hip dysplasia due to arthritic changes in the hip joint
- Grating detected with joint movement
- Decreased range of motion in the hip joints
- Loss of muscle mass in thigh muscles
- Enlargement of shoulder muscles due to more weight being exerted on front legs as dog tries to avoid weight on its hips, leading to extra work for the shoulder muscles and subsequent enlargement of these muscles

Elbow dysplasia
- Not all affected dogs will show signs when young

  - Sudden (acute) episode of elbow lameness due to advanced degenerative joint disease in a mature patient are common

  - Intermittent or persistent forelimb lameness that is aggravated by exercise; progresses from stiffness, and noticed only after the dog has been resting

  - Pain when extending or flexing the elbow

  - Tendency for dogs to hold the affected limb away from the body

  - Fluid build-up in the joint

  - Grating of bone and joint with movement may be detected with advanced degenerative joint disease

  - Diminished range of motion

Treatment
Treatment depends on the individual dog and the severity of the condition. In mild cases, you may never know that your dog has any dysplasia. If your dog begins to show stiffness or other signs of arthritis as he gets older, you can talk to your vet about mild painkillers, provide a heated, comfortable dog bed, and help your dog avoid stairs and other things that might overtax him. However, regular light exercise is good to keep the muscles in shape. Swimming is very good exercise for older dogs and dogs

with hip dysplasia. In rare cases a dog might require surgery, but this is not common.

k) Canine inherited demyelinative neuropathy (CIDN)
This is an inherited condition in Tibetan Mastiffs. It appears by the time puppies are six weeks old. There is no cure and puppies usually die by the time they are four months old. The condition affects the nervous system and the hindquarters become completely paralysed.

Note that these are health problems that have occurred in the breed. That doesn't mean they are common or that your Tibetan Mastiff will get any of them. Before getting a puppy you should talk to your breeder and ask about these conditions. Find out if the breeder is aware of them. Ask if his or her dogs have had any of these problems. In some cases there may be tests to determine if the problem is passed on to offspring. In other cases, there are no tests yet. Find out about possible health issues before you get a puppy.

First Aid for your Tibetan Mastiff

While it's important to work with your veterinarian, you should also be familiar with the basics of canine first aid. You can take several courses that will take you through more in-depth first aid but this section should get you started.

a) First Aid Kit

Every home that has a Tibetan Mastiff should have a first aid kit. Having a first aid kit will not only reduce the chance of having to go to the vet's office but will also give your dog precious minutes in a life-threatening situation.

To create a first aid kit, fill an easy-to-access Tupperware or backpack with the following:

Important Numbers

Tape important numbers to your container so you never have to search for the number during a crisis. Numbers to have on hand are:

- Your Veterinarian's Office
- Emergency Clinic -- also have the address to the clinic
- Poison Control Centre

Medicine

There are a number of medications that you can have on hand, which will help you manage a condition or treat it quickly. Always keep track of expiration dates on the medication in your first aid kit.

- Wound Disinfectant for cuts
- Sterile Saline for washing out wounds
- Antibiotic Cream for cuts, scrapes, etc.
- Cortisone Cream for itchy skin
- Ear Cleaning Solution
- Eye Wash Solution
- Antibiotic Eye Ointment

- Hydrogen Peroxide for vomiting (only use at the discretion of your vet)

- Activated Charcoal (only use at the discretion of your vet)

- Gas X or any gas medication to help prevent bloat

- Anti-diarrhea medication

- Benadryl for allergies (only use at the discretion of your vet)

Equipment
While you may not feel you need a lot of equipment, you should have the equipment listed below. Sometimes having the right equipment can mean your dog is treated at home and not at the vet's. Or it can save your dog's life.

- Magnifying glass

- Nail clippers

- Cotton balls

- Cotton swabs

- Cold packs
- Heat packs

- Thermometer

- Towels and blankets in case of emergency transport

- Scissors

- Penlight
- Styptic powder to stop bleeding
- Nail clippers
- Metal nail file
- Oral syringe
- Haemostat
- KY Jelly
- Eye Dropper
- Tweezers
- Disposable gloves
- Bitter Apple

In addition to these items, you should have a crate or pet carrier near your first aid kit for transporting your Tibetan Mastiff.

Bandages and Other
Finally, you will want to make sure that you have bandages and a few odds and ends in your first aid kit. Things you should have are:

- Karo Syrup
- Vitacal or other nutritional supplement
- Gatorade for rehydration

- Band-Aids
- Square Gauze
- Non-stick pads
- First aid tape
- Bandage rolls
- Vetwrap

Once you have all your supplies, place the kit in an easy to access area.

b) Dealing with an Emergency

Now that you have your first aid kit all ready for your Tibetan Mastiff, you are prepared for many of the little mishaps that life with a dog can bring. But are you ready for an emergency? Hopefully, the answer is yes. In this section we'll go over some of the things you should know.

Here are some tips for dealing with an emergency.

Tip Number 1: Be Calm and Cautious
Although the first reaction is to panic, remain calm so your dog can feel the strength coming from you. In addition, always be cautious with handling the dog when there's an emergency. If your Tibetan Mastiff is hurt or frightened, moving too roughly can injure him further or cause him to react.

Tip Number 2: Only Move Your Dog if Necessary
Make sure that you only move your dog if he needs to be moved.

Sometimes lifting a dog too soon can compound the injury. If you can, wrap him carefully in a blanket and then move him.

Tip Number Three: Use your Voice
Tibetan Mastiffs often have a very strong bond with their owners and will react to your voice. If you talk to the dog in a loving and gentle manner, the dog will pick up on your tone and relax. This will make first aid or seeking medical help easier.

Tip Number Four: Keep your Tibetan Mastiff Warm
Wrap your dog in a warm towel or apply a warm compress if your dog is unconscious or showing any signs of going into shock. By keeping your dog warm, you are less likely to complicate his condition.

Tip Number Five: Staunch Blood Loss
In the event of an injury with blood loss, make a compression bandage or manually compress the area to prevent as much blood loss as possible.

Remember that what you do in those first few minutes after a serious accident or emergency can mean the difference between life and death in some cases.

i. First Aid for Eye Injuries
When your Tibetan Mastiff has an eye injury, it is important to look at the type of injury. If there is something in the eye, carefully flush the eye with an eye wash. You may need to have someone hold your dog's head while you put the liquid in the eye.

If your dog has injured his eye and it is bleeding, take an eye dropper and carefully rinse the eyeball. You do not want to flush but simply moisten it. Once it is moistened, apply a compress gently over the eye. This will help staunch the bleeding and will keep the eye free from exposure.

Seek immediate veterinarian care after you have administered the first aid.

ii. First Aid for Seizures

If your Tibetan Mastiff has a seizure you should contact your veterinarian as soon as possible. There can be several reasons for a seizure.

During the seizure, don't hold your dog. They can be very scared during a seizure and may bite while having the seizure.

In addition to staying clear, remove any objects that he might hurt himself on, such as furniture. Finally, turn off any type of stimulation. Lights should be turned off, radios as well, and people should try to stay quiet.

While the seizure is happening, time it and write down when it started and when it ended. This is important in case there are recurring seizures.

After the seizure has stopped, comfort your dog. Wrap him in a warm blanket and then sit with him until he begins to act normal. Follow the directions of your vet and take him in for an examination.

iii. First Aid for Heat Stroke

With their thick coats, it is possible for Tibetan Mastiffs to develop heat stroke or heat exhaustion. To help prevent heat stroke, do not leave your dog outside when it's very hot. In addition, never leave a dog in a hot car.

If your Tibetan Mastiff does develop heat stroke, it is important to follow these steps:

1. Move the dog out of the hot area. Bring him to shade or inside.

2. Soak a towel with cold water.

3. Place the towel over the neck and head of your dog. Do not cover his eyes and keep his face clear of the fabric.

4. Repeat the process, wetting the towel down with cold water every few minutes.

5. If you can't get to a vet, pour water over the dog's hind legs and abdomen.

6. While you are pouring water, massage the legs and then push the water off of the dog. Keeping the water moving will help cool the dog more.

As soon as you are able to, take the dog to the veterinarian. Heat exhaustion needs to be treated with the help of a trained professional.

iv. First Aid for Fractures
Another emergency that will require veterinarian care, there is not a lot that you can do for your Tibetan Mastiff if there is a fracture. While some people will try to create a splint, that can cause more harm than good.

Instead, take the time to muzzle your dog to keep him from biting. Then make a sling from a towel and blanket and keep him secure. Do not press on his chest or touch the area where the fracture is.

Place a blanket over him to keep your dog warm, especially if he is going into shock.

Take your pet to the veterinarian's office immediately.

v. First Aid for Burns
In the event of a burn, as long as it is not a severe burn that covers a large portion of the dog's body, you can treat the burn at home. If it is severe or covers a large area, seek medical attention immediately.

For small burns, flush the burn area with large quantities of water until the burn starts to cool. You can use a burn relief ointment but make sure that it is not toxic if ingested.

vi. First Aid for Choking
Choking can be a very scary situation for dog owners and it can happen very quickly. If your dog is choking, be sure to act quickly but be mindful that a choking dog is more likely to bite.

When the dog is choking, carefully grab his muzzle. Open his mouth and look inside it. If you can see the object that is causing him to choke, take a pair of tweezers and carefully pull the object out.

It is very important to be careful when you are doing this as it is easy to push the object further back into the throat. If you are unable to get the object out, seek medical help immediately.

If the dog stops breathing or collapses, place your Tibetan Mastiff on his side. Place your hand over the rib cage and firmly strike the rib cage three to four times with the flat of your palm. Repeat as necessary on your journey to the vet.

While this may have no effect, administering this technique could force the air out of the lungs and force the obstruction out of your dog's throat.

vii. First Aid for Shock
Another emergency that needs medical help, shock should be managed as you take your dog to the vet.

Wrap your dog in a warm blanket and keep him warm. Also, lay him down and try to keep his head level with the rest of his body. Stay calm and comfort your dog to help minimize his discomfort.

viii. First Aid for Bleeding
If your Tibetan Mastiff has an injury that has resulted in bleeding, it is important to staunch the flow of blood. Using a thick gauze pad, apply pressure to the wound. The pressure will aid in stimulating the clotting mechanism of blood. If it is a minor injury, the bleeding will usually stop in a few minutes and you can then move to cleaning the wound.

If it is severe, keep the pressure on the dog's wound. Wrap him in a blanket or use a heat pad to keep him warm. This will help prevent shock as you take him to the veterinarian for treatment.

ix. First Aid for Poisoning
Finally, if your dog is exposed to poison, it is important to immediately call poison control and/or your vet. They will guide you through the steps to take depending on the poison he has ingested. In the case of some toxins, you may be advised to administer active charcoal. In cases of consuming poisons, hydrogen peroxide may be recommended to induce vomiting.

If it is contact through skin or eyes, follow the directions on the container with the poison. Wash the area or flush it with water.

c) CPR

CPR should only be used in the event that your dog is not breathing. If he is, do not administer CPR or you could cause more harm than good.

With CPR, follow these steps:

1. Remain calm.

2. Get someone to call your veterinarian.

3. Check the condition of your Tibetan Mastiff. Is he unconscious?

4. Open your dog's mouth and pull out his tongue until it is lying flat. Check to see if there is an obstruction. If there is, see the section on choking.

5. If there isn't, close your Tibetan Mastiff's mouth and hold it closed. Place your mouth on his nose and breath.

6. Watch the chest and breathe until it expands.

7. Pause and count to 5, then repeat with a breath.

8. Check your dog's heartbeat. The best place to do this is right above the pad on his front paw.

9. Lay him on his right side.

10. Slip your one hand under his right side in the lower half of his chest.

11. Place your hand, palm down over the lower half of his left side. This is where the heart is on a dog.

12. Press down about a half inch into the chest. (The depth varies with 1 inch for medium sized dogs, more for larger, less for smaller.)

13. Press down repeatedly, about 100 to 150 times per minute for small dogs, 80 to 120 times per minute for larger animals.

14. If you are using rescue breathing, have someone help you. One person can press the chest for 4 to 5 seconds for every single breath.

15. Repeat until you can feel a heartbeat or do it while someone else is driving you and your Tibetan Mastiff to the vet.

Although the information in this chapter will help you and your Tibetan Mastiff, please remember that it should never replace the advice and care of a veterinarian.

Chapter Eleven: Breeding your Tibetan Mastiff

Breeding your Tibetan Mastiff is an important decision that every dog owner should make before they purchase a puppy. While we often think of breeding after the purchase, by choosing to breed beforehand, you can ensure that you are starting with the very best dog you can find.

Remember to read the chapter on choosing a puppy in this book. One thing that will help you is to find a mentor in the breed before you decide to breed your dog. Breeding a Tibetan Mastiff is a constant learning experience and it will help you to know someone in the breed who has years of experience.

This chapter will provide you with tips on choosing the right dogs for your breeding program, how and when to breed, the simple facts about birthing a puppy, and the schedule for raising puppies.

Choosing dogs to breed

The very first thing that you should do before deciding to breed your Tibetan Mastiff is to choose the right dogs. While every dog can be bred, not every dog should be bred. It is important to really understand the breed standard of the Tibetan Mastiff before you breed.

If you are interested in breeding professionally, you will probably want to find a "breeding pair" – a male and female Tibetan Mastiff. However, most people who breed as a hobby or breed to show their dogs look for the best male or female dog they can find. They usually seek the best female dog if they want to breed a litter. That's because they can use stud dogs owned by other breeders without tying themselves to the same male forever.

If you have a good female dog, you will likely want to choose a different mate for her each time. That way you can see what kind of puppies she produces with different dogs or different bloodlines. If you are serious about being a dog breeder, you need to think in terms of generations. Having two or three litters from your girl from different bloodlines could give you the best start for the future, assuming you will be keeping a puppy from a litter for yourself.

In general, when you are choosing a dog for breeding, you want to look at the following:

Health
Dogs should be healthy and in good condition. They should be in proportionate weight for their build and also pass a health test from your vet. They should be free of disease so there is no risk of that disease being passed along to the young.

If the vet voices any concerns over the health of the dogs, wait to breed them until they are in better health or choose different dogs.

Clearances
Clearances are very important to ensure the health of your puppies and the lifelong health of any dog you produce. Tibetan Mastiff have several hereditary diseases so the health clearances you should get on your dogs are:

- Eyes Certified by a board-certified ACVO Ophthalmologist

- OFA or PennHip certification for Hip Dysplasia

- OFA evaluation for Autoimmune Thyroiditis

- OFA evaluation for elbow dysplasia is optional in the breed.

In addition to these clearances, you should have the dogs tested for brucellosis, which is a canine STD. Any dog that is being bred should be clear. Brucellosis can cause sterility in both males and females and can cause the dam to abort the puppies.

Registration
Before buying any dog for breeding, you should make sure the dog is registered with the kennel club you desire, or eligible to be registered.

Temperament
Temperament is as important as health when it comes to breeding. Studies have proven that temperament is a hereditary trait so it is important to breed dogs with a sound temperament. If you have a dog with aggression or skittishness, it is recommended that you do not breed the dog.

Bloodlines
Another factor that you want to take into account is the blood line. Is it a strong pedigree? When considering pedigrees for breeding it is particularly important to have a mentor or someone you trust give you some advice. Linebreeding, outcrossing, and other breeding theories, as well as just reading pedigrees takes some practice to understand them.

Age
Something that is very important with breeding is the age of the dogs. Females should be no younger than 18 months of age for

breeding and males shouldn't be younger than 15 months of age. Ideally, you won't breed a male or female before they have had at least preliminary hip x-rays so you can be reasonably certain they do not have hip dysplasia.

Some health clearances cannot be done until the dog is older.

On the other end of the age spectrum, you should not breed a bitch after she is 7 years of age. Males can be bred for many years after that; however, the quality and quantity of sperm can be affected by age.

Physical Traits
Finally, you will want to choose dogs according to their physical traits. While the dogs you select should be good examples of the breed, you should look at what each dog can bring to their future puppies.

For instance, if both dogs have excellent ears according to the breed standard, the odds are very high that the puppies will inherit those ears. A good coat on a female may be passed on to the puppies, even if the male has a coat that isn't as good. A good body shape on the male may be passed on to the puppies and so on.

Choosing complementary traits will only improve your puppies and your lines. While many people promote showing, it is not a prerequisite for breeding. However, showing your dogs does have benefits for breeding dogs. It puts you in touch with a community of reputable breeders. It allows you to see many Tibetan Mastiffs and compare traits. It keeps you informed about dog matters. So, it has advantages for anyone interested in breeding dogs.

Before you do make that final decision about which dogs to

breed, it is important to remember that breeding is a responsibility. There is often very little money to be earned when doing it properly and it is a full time commitment.

While the dam will help with the care, there is a lot to be done during those 8 (or more) weeks that you will be raising puppies at home. In addition, breeders should be prepared to rehome any of their puppies if they are returned for some reason.

Breeding is not for the faint of heart by any means but one thing is certain: cuddling a newborn Tibetan Mastiff in your arms is worth all the work, money and commitment.

Before breeding your female dog, we recommend that you make sure she is up-to-date on her vaccinations. The mother dog will be able to pass along temporary immunity to common dog diseases to her puppies when they are born so you want to make sure her own immunity is at maximum. In the UK and Europe we also recommend that bitches receive the canine herpes virus vaccination before breeding. Canine herpes virus is extremely widespread, affecting up to 90 percent of all dogs. It is harmless to most adult dogs but, under stress, it can kill newborn puppies. The vaccine is very helpful in protecting the newborns. Unfortunately, this vaccine is not available at this time in the United States.

Breeding your Tibetan Mastiff

Now that you have chosen the dogs you wish to breed, it is time to breed your dog. While it may seem like a simple thing, breeding a Tibetan Mastiff can be challenging. Dogs usually know how to mate (usually), but there is a lot you need to know to have a successful litter.

The Heat

When a female dog reaches sexual maturity, she will begin what is known as a heat. A heat or heat cycle is when the female will begin bleeding and will be ready to accept the male within a few days. For Tibetan Mastiff, the first heat is usually between six months and a year; however, a dog should never be bred on her first heat or before the age of 18 months to 2 years.

With heat cycles, some females will take longer to have their first heat and it is not uncommon for a Tibetan Mastiff to be closer to a year of age or even up to 2 years when she has her first heat. As a "primitive" breed, Tibetan Mastiffs still retain traits that are closer to the dog's wolf ancestors. One of these traits is the fact that females of the breed commonly only come in season once per year, usually in the fall. Most domestic dogs today come in season slightly more often (ranging from every six to nine months for many breeds). For this reason, most Tibetan Mastiff puppies are conceived in the fall and born in the winter.

With heat cycles, signs of the heat begin before the discharge. Often the vulva begins to swell and the female will begin licking her back end and vulva more. In addition, she may be urinating more frequently and if you have any male dogs in the home, you may notice them paying more attention to her than usual.

The female will begin to have a bloody discharge and this can vary in heaviness between females and even heats. Some females have very little discharge and other females have a lot. **Females are not ready to breed at this time**. The discharge will gradually become paler until it is a straw colour. This usually takes around 2 to 11 days. This is when the female is ready to breed. Young male dogs may not be able to tell the difference but experienced stud dogs often won't bother spending much time with a female until she is actually ready to breed.

The entire heat cycle lasts about 3 weeks but it is important to not let the female near a male until about 4 weeks after the start of her heat. If you are planning on breeding her, breeding will take place about 9 to 11 days after her heat starts.

Natural or Artificial?

When you are breeding, you can choose between allowing the dogs to breed naturally or doing an AI (Artificial Insemination) breeding. Many breeders learn how to do AIs themselves, however, in the event of frozen sperm, you would need to have the AI done by a veterinarian, specifically a reproductive veterinarian. Frozen sperm is often shipped to a breeder by another breeder from a long distance, at considerably expense. You don't want to take any chances that the insemination might fail.

Natural breeding is when you allow the male dog to mount the female and achieve a tie. This is often the more preferred way to breed.

With AI, the sperm is delivered to the vagina through a sterilized tube. There are several reasons why you would use AI and these are:

- Stud dog is too far away.
- A dominant female who will not allow a male to mount.
- Inexperienced stud dog.
- A persistent hymen in a bitch.

- Size incompatibility

AI is less likely to spread an STD but it usually accounts for smaller litter sizes. Also, it is important to properly judge when ovulation occurs, which can be difficult and is usually done with progesterone testing by your vet.

Many breeders use AI with fresh semen, even when the stud dog is on the premises. This is done to avoid any injury to the stud dog and to avoid any chance of passing disease.

When to Breed

You have the stud dog, a bitch in heat and you have made the decision to go with a natural tie. Terrific, you are ready to start breeding soon ... but maybe not right away.

Breeding times differs from female to female, although the general rule of thumb is between days 9 and 11. If you have the male in the home, you can begin breeding as soon as the female starts accepting him.

The rule of thumb, however, is to breed every other day. This gives the sperm time to recover in numbers and you will have better sperm numbers.

If you don't have a male, you can do progesterone testing to try to narrow down when your female is most fertile. Progesterone testing is done with a blood test, however, you can also do a vaginal smear, although this is not as accurate.

When using progesterone testing, follow the guidelines of your veterinarian.

Although testing the dog is an excellent way to identify if your female dog is ready to be bred, you can also see this with her behaviour. A female that is ready to be bred will exhibit the following:

- Vaginal discharge will turn to a light pink or straw colour.
- The female will back up into the male.
- She will hold her tail to the side. This is known as flagging.
- She will be playful with the male.
- She will stand still when the male is sniffing her.
- She won't attack the male when he tries to mount her.

When you see these signs, your female is ready to be bred. Even with these signs, however, progesterone testing can be more accurate for determining the exact right time for mating. There is a spike in the LH (luteinizing hormone) 48 hours prior to ovulation. This spike will trigger the progesterone levels to begin rising, signalling the best times for breeding. After the LH surge and the rise in progesterone, do a natural breeding three days later, for example. The sperm in fresh semen can survive 5 to 7 days in the female dog's uterus.

Artificial insemination using fresh chilled semen can be used four days after the rise in progesterone. Sperm in chilled semen survive 48 to 72 hours after insemination.

Artificial insemination using frozen semen can be used five days after the progesterone surge. Sperm in frozen semen only survives 24 hours once it is deposited in the uterus by surgical means after insemination.

The Act of Breeding

When your female is ready to be bred, it is time to let the dogs do their job. During this time, you should allow the stud dog and the bitch to be together. Never leave them unattended as injuries can occur if the female attacks the male or she becomes scared.

The stud dog will spend some time sniffing the rear of the female and he may begin to lick the vulva. The female will stand still and will move her tail out of the way. She will also back into the male.

Note, if you have a maiden bitch or an inexperienced stud dog, you can have success without intervening, but things often go much better if you are on hand to assist. Inexperienced stud dogs can sometimes be so excited that they will mount the wrong end of the girl, for example. Maiden girls are not always sure what that pesky boy has in mind. The dogs usually figure things out but if you have invested a lot of money in a stud fee or driven a long way with your girl, sometimes it helps if you or the stud dog owner lend a guiding hand. You can hold the bitch in position or guide the boy in the right direction, for example.

If you have an experienced bitch and/or stud dog, they usually know what they are doing and things go smoothly and quickly when the time is right.

As the male builds excitement, he will mount the female, wrapping his front legs around the hips of the female. He will begin to thrust against the female and his penis will enter the vulva.

During this action, the glans penis will come out of the sheaf, which is a bright red organ. The penis will extend into the vulva until the dog locks with the female. Once the lock happens, the male and female cannot be separated. Do not try to separate them as you can hurt both the male and the female.

Once he is locked, the male will lift his leg over the rear of the female and then turn so they are standing with their back ends together. The penis will bend but will still be inserted in the vulva. Dogs will remain locked for 10 to 30 minutes until the penis loses some of its swelling so it is released from the lock.

One myth that abounds is that a female cannot get pregnant if there is no tie. This is not true. When the dog is thrusting, sperm is released. The fluid that is released when they are locked is very low in sperm and is used to push the sperm through the cervix. Only allow your dogs to mate once per day and then wait a day before you breed again.

Is She Pregnant

The gestational period for dogs is between the 63 to 65 days after the time of first breeding, however, you can have some additional or fewer days depending on the individual dog and breeding. If you have used progesterone testing, whelping is nearly always exactly 63 days after ovulation. Even if you have bred your dogs late in the heat, you can count on 63 days from ovulation rather than from the date of the breeding.

One of the biggest worries that breeders go through is whether a dog is pregnant. This is very difficult to determine because a female dog goes through the same hormone changes whether she is pregnant or not. In fact, even a female who has not been bred can present the symptoms of pregnancy.

During the first month, you will notice very few signs. The female may have morning sickness where her appetite decreases, however, some females are not affected at all.

After the first 30 days, the dog will begin to show some symptoms. Symptoms of pregnancy are:

- Nipple Growth
- Pinking of the Nipples
- Decreased Appetite early on
- Increased Appetite around week 6
- Clinginess and other behaviour changes
- Pear shape of the abdomen
- Weight gain

At 30 to 35 days, you can have an ultrasound done to confirm pregnancy. Numbers are not usually given during ultrasounds as it is very difficult to count the puppies. Experienced vets and breeders can often palpate a bitch's abdomen and feel puppies. At 30 days puppies are about the size of walnuts. After this time they can't be felt again for several weeks. After 45 days gestation, an x-ray can be done and the puppies can be counted at that time. It is important to note that sometimes counts are wrong since puppies will hide in the x-ray. It is a good idea to have an x-ray done so you will know how many puppies to expect. This helps you know when your girl is finished whelping.

During pregnancy you can continue to feed your female her normal dog food for the first six weeks. After this time you can begin to increase her food. You can add some pre-natal vitamins to her diet but do **not** add any additional calcium or other supplements at this time. You can switch her to an all life stage dog food or a puppy food at this time since she will be using the extra calories as the puppies develop. Once the puppies are born, you can feed your female dog as much as she wants to eat, especially if she has several puppies. She will need the extra calories to produce milk.

Whelping your Pups

So your female is pregnant and the time is drawing closer to when you will be whelping her puppies. This is an exciting time but it is also a busy time for you. It is very important to have all your supplies ready and to begin preparing for the puppies a few weeks before their arrival.

Whelping Supplies

The first thing that is important to have on hand are the whelping supplies. These are essential for helping your puppies and mother. In the best case scenario, you will need to interact very little with the labour. In the worst case, you could be looking at having to rush your pregnant dog to the vet clinic for an emergency c-section.

In addition, even an easy whelping can result in puppies in distress so it is important to have the tools on hand to help the puppies. Things you will need in your whelping supplies are:

- *Whelping Box:* This should be a square box that the mother can deliver and raise her puppies in. You can make the box yourself or you can purchase pre-made whelping boxes. The box does need to be sturdy and good quality. This will be the puppies' home for the next few weeks.

- *Blankets:* Have a lot of blankets on hand for your whelping box. Labour is messy and that means you have to exchange the bedding in the whelping box several times during labour.

- *Newspaper:* In addition to blankets, have a large amount of newspaper to put down during the whelping process. Again, you are going to be going through a lot of it. You can also get end rolls from your local newspaper. These are clean paper rolls without the ink. They aren't nearly as messy as newspaper.

- *Basket:* A laundry basket or Tupperware container to put the puppies in when the female is birthing another puppy.

- *Hot Water Bottles:* Water bottles are needed for the basket so puppies can stay warm when they are not with their mother. Puppies will cuddle up to the water bottles if they are cold and will move away if they are too warm. You can also use a heating pad, but wrap it with a towel so the puppies don't get burned on it.

- *Scale:* Have a kitchen scale so you can properly weigh each puppy as it is born. This will be a tool you use throughout the time the litter is with you since you will want to weigh the puppies on a regular basis.

- *Notebook and Pens:* Create a notebook that charts the progress of each individual puppy. Start with the puppies' sex, identifier, date of birth, presentation at birth, time born, colouration and weight. This will help you keep track of each puppy.

- *Identifier:* This can be yarn, puppy collars, or nail polish for their nails. Basically, it is anything that you can use to identify each puppy. Use the yarn like a collar on each puppy so you can identify each individual puppy right from birth. Use the same collar colour for that puppy throughout the 8 weeks that you have the puppies.

In addition to those items, have the following items available in a kit. Be sure to sterilize all of the instruments such as the scissors and haemostats:

- Sharp Scissors
- Haemostats
- Surgical Gloves
- Iodine Swabs
- Alcohol Swabs
- Lubricating Jelly such as K-Y

- Digital Thermometer
- Vaseline
- Nursing Bottles for Puppies
- Liquid Puppy Vitamins
- Puppy Formula
- Energizing Glucose Drops
- Bulb Syringe

Place all of the items into an easy to access container and have it close to your whelping box.

Before Labour

As you know, the gestation period for dogs is about 63 days, give or take a few days. However, it is important to monitor your dog during the days leading up to the delivery. Around day 56 to 58, the female should start searching for a nesting site. Encourage her to nest in the whelping box by sitting next to it and calmly petting her. Don't discourage her scratching at the bedding as this is normal.

In addition to this, you should start taking her temperature about a week before her due date. The average temperature of your female will be between 99 to 101°F (37.22 to 38.33°C). Mark down her temperature each day and, closer to the due date, start checking her temperature several times per day.

The reason why we are watching the temperature is because we are waiting for a temperature spike and then drop. About 48 hours before labour, her temperature will have a spike up to about 101.5°F (38.6°C) or higher. Within 24 hours after that, the temperature will drop. Once it gets to below 98°F (36.7°C), you will have between 12 to 24 hours before the litter is expected.

First Stage Labour

When she has her final temp drop, you will start to notice a number of signs that your female is going into labour. For about 2 to 12 hours, your female will become restless. She may start to nest even more than she did before, or she may become very stressed wanting to wander around the house.

You may see some shivering and she will probably change positions frequently. Her eyes will dilate and she will watch you and want to be with you. Try to stay near the whelping box so she can settle in.

She may lose her appetite during this time and it is not uncommon for your Tibetan Mastiff female to vomit. Also, she may try to go to the bathroom and not be able to. This is caused by the pressure building up in her stomach.

If you take your Tibetan Mastiff outside to go to the bathroom, keep her on a leash and check the spot where she squatted. It is not uncommon for puppies to be born outside.

Finally, you may see some mucus being discharged from the vulva.

Second Stage of Labour

During the second stage of labour, your female should start digging at her bedding even more. You will also notice your Tibetan Mastiff looking at her back end more frequently and she may start licking her vulva.

Shivering is more noticeable and she will have periods where she is panting heavily. You may be able to see mild contractions going across her belly or you may feel a tightening of her stomach.

Again, your Tibetan Mastiff may vomit and she may ask to go outside more frequently. Remember to stay with her when she goes to the bathroom to make sure a pup isn't born outside.

At this time, if the discharge turns to a dark green colour, seek medical help. Dark green discharge is normal but only after a puppy is born. If it is before, it can indicate a life-threatening problem for both your bitch and your litter.

Third Stage of Labour

This is the stage of labour when the puppies begin to be whelped. During this time, the contractions will become stronger and you will be able to see them. They will also occur closer together.

Your Tibetan Mastiff female may vomit during this time and you will notice that she will begin pushing and grunting. Some females will squat when they have their puppies, others will lay on their side so let the female decide how she is going to birth the puppy.

As she is pushing, you will see a membrane sac filled with water and the puppy come out of the vulva. Puppies are born in their own sac and it may burst while being delivered or as the female breaks it.

In addition, puppies are born both front feet first and breech, with their tail or back feet presented first. The puppy is followed by the afterbirth. Females often eat the afterbirth and it contains material to stimulate milk production. Count each afterbirth after the puppies are born to make sure each one is expelled. A retained afterbirth can cause a serious infection and lead to complications for your female.

Puppies are usually born in quick succession of two or three puppies, then you will have a wait of about an hour or so before additional puppies are born.

The process of birthing can last up to 24 hours, depending on the size of the litter.

If you find that the female is pushing for longer than 30 minutes without seeing a puppy, contact your veterinarian and follow his advice. It could mean a puppy is caught.

Also, if there is a long period of time between puppies, contact your veterinarian, especially if you are expecting more puppies.

When the puppies are born, allow them to nurse from their mother between births. Every time she is ready to push, remove the puppies to your basket. This keeps her from being distracted by the puppies and she is less likely to sit on the puppy or hurt it. Try to let her do the work herself. If you get too involved, you could cause her to stop labouring. Only get involved if she looks like she needs help.

In between puppies, weigh the puppy that was recently born, jot down all the notes on the puppy and place an identifier collar on the puppy.

Watching a litter being born is a very exciting thing but make sure you are prepared for any problems. Also, keep the whelping room quiet and calm.

It is also important to note that in the weeks after giving birth, the gland that is responsible for regulating the parathyroid hormone, which in turn regulates the amount of calcium which is stored within the mother, can become depleted.

When the bitch's milk starts to come in, and the demand for calcium suddenly is increased, the parathyroid gland is unable to respond quickly enough for her needs to be fully met. This can lead to her body contracting convulsively, which effectively will limit her movement. This condition is known as eclampsia.

Once diagnosed with eclampsia, the new mother will be prescribed calcium supplementation. Alternatively, foods such as Cottage Cheese, Goats Milk, or Mature Cheddar will also help in supporting her to heal through this phase.

If your female becomes fatigued during delivery or seems to be stalled, you can provide her with some vanilla ice cream for energy.

After whelping, be sure she eats and has plenty of fresh water. You can offer her some chicken or broth if her appetite is off. She should soon be hungry again since she will be nursing a litter of puppies.

Raising Pups

Raising pups is a fun activity and for the first few weeks, the mother does the majority of the work. She will clean the puppies and feed them. However, it doesn't mean that you have nothing to do -- you will be very busy with your own chores. Below is a chart of what you need to do with the puppies while they are growing.

Age	Puppy Development	Chores List
Week 1	The puppies sleep the majority of the time. When they are awake, they will crawl and squirm towards warmth and milk. The puppies will have their eyes and ears closed and are very helpless at this age.	▪ Chart Weight twice a day ▪ Trim nails at the end of the week. ▪ Handle the puppies daily to check their health and start neurological stimulation ▪ Clean the bedding daily. ▪ Monitor the mom and her health. ▪ Keep whelping box at about 85°F (29.4°C)
Week 2	Puppies are beginning to move around more and they are awake for	▪ Trim nails at the end of the week. ▪ Hold the puppies

	longer periods. Eyes will begin to open at day 8 to 10, ears will open near the end of week 2 or beginning of week 3.	in different positions. ⬛ Monitor the mother and her health. ⬛ Clean bedding daily. ⬛ Weigh puppies once a day.
Week 3	Eyes and ears will be open by the end of this week and they will become more active. They will start trying to walk and will be able to go to the bathroom without stimulation from mother. They will begin to play and their little teeth are erupting.	⬛ Continue to handle the puppies. ⬛ Trim nails at end of the week. ⬛ Begin socializing the puppy to things such as grooming items. ⬛ Weigh puppies every other day. ⬛ Monitor the mother and her health. ⬛ Begin weaning process. Start with milk replacer once a day for two days. Then add a mushy food once per day. ⬛ Clean bedding daily

Week 4 During this week, the puppies will be more playful and will begin growling. They will also be eating food and while they may nurse occasionally, mom will have less to do with them but should still be with them a lot. Cleaning up poop will be your job as soon as they start eating things other than their mother's milk.

- Continue to handle the puppies.
- Trim nails at end of the week.
- Begin socializing the puppy to other things such as noises and other animals in your home.
- Weigh puppies every other day.
- Monitor the mother and her health.
- Shift the food to an oatmeal like consistency, add one extra meal a day.
- Clean bedding daily

Week 5 Puppies are more alert and they will be active. You will start to notice pack order and may even see sexual play. Puppies

- Weigh puppies two to three times each week.
- Reduce the mother's diet to stop

	will grow quickly during this time.	her milk production. ⬚ Start reducing the amount of liquid in the puppies' food. ⬚ Continue to handle the puppies. ⬚ Trim nails at end of the week. ⬚ Continue socializing the puppies to a range of stimuli. ⬚ Clean bedding daily.
Week 6	Puppies are developing quickly and they are developing their own personalities. Mom will be with the puppies less at this stage.	⬚ Give each puppy alone time. ⬚ Weigh the puppies weekly. ⬚ Continue reducing the amount of liquid in the puppies' food. ⬚ Continue to handle the puppies. ⬚ Trim nails at end of the week. ⬚ Continue socializing the puppies to a range of stimuli. ⬚ Clean bedding

daily.

Week 7	Puppies will be able to hear and see fully at this stage. They will be very inquisitive and can get into some problems.	▫ Give each puppy alone time. ▫ Weigh the puppies weekly. ▫ Puppies should be fully weaned and on puppy food. ▫ Continue to handle the puppies. ▫ Trim nails at end of the week. ▫ Continue socializing the puppies to a range of stimuli. ▫ Clean bedding daily.

Week 8

Puppies are at the age where they can start going to their new homes. This is the week when a fear period can occur so make sure you do not stress them too much.

- Give each puppy alone time.
- Weigh the puppies weekly.
- Trim nails at end of the week.
- Continue socializing the puppies to a range of stimuli.
- Clean bedding daily.
- Start training puppies that have not left for their new home.

Raising a litter of puppies is a lot of work so before you breed your dog, it's important to do a lot of research and be ready for the commitment. Any breeder will also tell you that it's advisable to have homes lines up for the puppies before you breed, or at least to know how you will place your puppies. Tibetan Mastiff puppies may be highly desirable but it's still necessary to let people know you are breeding a litter. You will want to make sure your puppies are going to good homes after you have put so much work into breeding the litter and raising them. Most breeders have a waiting list and take deposits on their puppies when they are born.

Chapter Twelve: Saying Goodbye To Your Tibetan Mastiff

Saying goodbye to a beloved friend is never easy. That's true whether you have lived with your Tibetan Mastiff since he was a puppy or if you brought him home as an adult dog. It's easy to fall in love with a dog, especially a dog who devotes himself to protecting you and your family and home.

Tibetan Mastiffs do tend to live longer than many breeds but one of the great drawbacks of having a pet is that we usually outlive them. Even if your dog lives to be 14 or 15 years old, there may come a time when you have to consider making a difficult decision.

In some cases an ageing dog will simply slip quietly away in his sleep or die suddenly. You may not have time to say goodbye or even to think about your dog's last days. But many dogs, as they get older, will start to have a few nagging health problems. They will slow down, gain weight, sleep more. You will notice their greying muzzle and perhaps signs of arthritis. All of these signs are indications that you should treasure every day with your dog because you may not have that much time left together.

Vet care for older dogs

As your Tibetan Mastiff starts to get older you and your vet can begin to make some plans for him. By the time he is seven or eight years old, your veterinarian will probably suggest a senior exam for your dog. This involves some bloodwork, urinalysis, and other tests so your vet will have some good baseline readings for your dog when he is younger and healthy. Should your dog get sick, your vet will have readings for comparison. Your vet will probably want to run the same kind of tests every year to see if there are any changes in your dog's health. This is a good way to catch any health problems early – before they become very serious.

You can also help with your older dog's care by checking him for lumps and bumps every time you groom him. Some fatty lumps and other things are not unusual as a dog gets older, but you will still probably want your vet to look at any odd changes in your dog's skin or other changes that you notice. Finding a problem early means it can be removed or treated and your dog stands a much better chance or recovering.

Saying goodbye

Eventually, we all have to say goodbye to the dogs we love. If you are having a dog euthanized ("put to sleep"), it's often best to take a friend with you to the veterinarian's offices. This is a very emotional, difficult experience and a friend can help you get through it. Some vets will come to your home to administer the injection which can be easier for your dog and you.

Some veterinarians can take care of a dog's remains but many owners prefer to do this themselves. There are pet cemeteries and services that will cremate animals, depending on where you live. Some owners find comfort in keeping their dog's ashes in an urn close by. In some rural areas you can still bury your dog on your own property so you can visit often.

Epitaph to a Dog
By George Gordon Lord Byron

Near this Spot

are deposited the Remains of one
who possessed Beauty without Vanity,
Strength without Insolence,
Courage without Ferocity,
and all the virtues of Man without his Vices.

This praise, which would be unmeaning Flattery
if inscribed over human Ashes,
is but a just tribute to the Memory of
Boatswain, a Dog
who was born in Newfoundland May 1803
and died at Newstead Nov. 18th, 1808

Rainbow Bridge

Just this side of heaven is a place called Rainbow Bridge.

When an animal dies that has been especially close to someone here, that pet goes to Rainbow Bridge. There are meadows and hills for all of our special friends so they can run and play together. There is plenty of food, water and sunshine, and our friends are warm and comfortable.

All the animals who had been ill and old are restored to health and vigor. Those who were hurt or maimed are made whole and strong again, just as we remember them in our dreams of days and times gone by. The animals are happy and content, except for one small thing; they each miss someone very special to them, who had to be left behind.

They all run and play together, but the day comes when one suddenly stops and looks into the distance. His bright eyes are intent. His eager body quivers. Suddenly he begins to run from the group, flying over the green grass, his legs carrying him faster and faster.

You have been spotted, and when you and your special friend finally meet, you cling together in joyous reunion, never to be parted again. The happy kisses rain upon your face; your hands again caress the beloved head, and you look once more into the trusting eyes of your pet, so long gone from your life but never absent from your heart.

Then you cross Rainbow Bridge together....

Author unknown...

Grief

Many pet owners suffer profound grief after the death of a pet. Unfortunately, they may have family and friends who do not understand their attachment to their pet. Many people have feelings for a pet like a member of the family. Losing that pet can be devastating. Going through grief surrounded by people who don't understand your loss can make your pain even worse.

If you are in this situation, or feeling sad and depressed after losing your pet, there are support groups with other pet owners who understand how you feel. You can check online to find some of these groups and we will list some in the Resources section at the back of this book. You can also check your local newspapers and other local sources for support groups. Many cities have pet loss support groups. Even if your town doesn't have a group devoted to pet loss, you can consider joining a group that discusses other kinds of loss, or talk to other pet owners who have also lost pets. They will understand what you are going through. You are definitely not alone.

Believe it or not, the feeling of loss will lessen and one day you will feel like having another dog again.

Chapter Thirteen: Common Terms

So you are interested in dogs and the Tibetan Mastiff? While most of the vocabulary dealing with dogs is the same as with any other animal, there are a few terms that you should know.

In this chapter, we'll cover some common terms that you may encounter as you enjoy life with your Tibetan Mastiff.

Agility: The Tibetan Mastiff thoroughly enjoys the sport of Dog Agility. This is a sport in which the dog handler guides and instructs the dog through a course of obstacles while being timed. Accuracy through this obstacle course is paramount. The dogs must complete the obstacle course without a leash or toys (or food) as incentives. The handler can only use voice, movement and various body signals in order to direct the dog.

Acquired Immunity: when a dog has developed antibodies that enables it to resist a disease. Acquired Immunity is often seen in newborn puppies as they get antibodies from their dam. It is also seen after vaccinations.

Acute Disease: refers to a disease or illness that manifests quickly.

Adoption: to take an animal or person in as your own. Is commonly used to describe bringing in a dog from a shelter or rescue but can also be used when purchasing a puppy.

Afterbirth: is a term used to describe the foetal membranes and placenta that is expelled after the birth of a puppy.

Agent: a person who trains, works or shows a dog. Also known as a handler.

Agility: a dog sport where the dogs will navigate through obstacles during a timed event. Tibetan Mastiff do very well in agility sports.

Albino: a genetic condition where an animal is born with white hair and pink eyes.

Allergen: a particle that triggers an allergic reaction. Found in dog hair, or specifically in a protein that is found in dog dander.

Almond eyes: eyes that have an elongated shape.

Alpha: the top dog in a social pack, usually the most dominant dog. Also refers to a form of training.

Alter: a term used to describe neutering or spaying.

Amble: used to describe a gait where the dog's legs on either side move almost as a pair.

Anal Glands: sacks or glands that are found on either side of the anus. All dogs use the substance secreted by the gland to mark territory.

Anestrus: the period of time between heats in female dogs.

Ankle: found in the hind legs, it is the area between the second thigh and metatarsus where there is a collection of bones. Also known as the hock.

Anterior: the front of the dog.

Apron: refers to longer hair on the chest, also known as the frill.

Arm: refers to the area between the shoulder and elbow of the dog's front legs.

Articulation: refers to the area where bones meet.

Artificial Insemination: used during breeding, it refers to using artificial means to place semen into the bitch's reproductive tract.

Asymptomatic: when a dog has a disease but is not exhibiting symptoms.

Awn hairs: seen on dogs with double coats, it is the section of undercoat that is long and has a coarse texture to it. It should be slightly longer than the downy undercoat but shorter than the outer coat.

Back: the area on the dog that extends from the shoulders to the rump of the dog.

Back crossing: refers to the act of breeding a dog to its parent.

Backyard Breeder: refers to a breeder who breeds dogs for profit with little care for the health of the dogs and puppies. A slur.

Bad Mouth: when a dog has crooked teeth.

Balance: used to describe the symmetry of the dog as well as its proportion.

Bandy Legs: refers to legs that bend outward.

Barrel: refers to the area around the ribs of a dog.

Barrel Hocks: refers to legs where the hock turns outward, which makes the feet turn inward. Also known as spread hocks.

Beefy: when a dog has too much weight in his hindquarters.

Behaviour Modification: using training and conditioning to control, alter or teach specific behaviours.

Bitch: a common term used to describe a female dog.

Bite: when a dog places his teeth on something. Also used to describe the position of the upper and lower teeth when the dog has his mouth closed.

Blocky: when the dog has a square like shape to his head.

Blooded: refers to a dog with a pedigree that comes from a good breeding.

Bloodline: the pedigree of the dog.

Blunt Muzzle: when a dog has a square shaped muzzle.

Board: when the dog is placed in a location where the care, feeding and housing of the dog is paid for. Usually used when owners are on vacation.

Body Length: measured from the front of the breastbone to the pelvis to identify how long a dog is.

Booster Vaccination: injections given to a dog to boost the immunity they have to specific diseases. Usually given on a yearly basis.

Bossy: when a dog has shoulder muscles that have been over developed.

Brace: refers to two dogs that are presented as a pair. They should be of the same breed.

Break: when there is a change in coloration between the puppy and adult coat.

Breastbone: the area on the chest where 8 bones connect to form the area.

Breech Birth: the presentation of the puppy at birth. In breech, the puppy comes out hind end first. Breech birth is very common in dogs and does not usually cause a problem.

Breeches: fur on the upper thighs that is longer and fringe like. Also known as pants, culottes and trousers.

Breed: refers to a group of dogs that share common characteristics, traits and gene pool.

Breed Club: refers to a group of enthusiasts dedicated to a specific breed.

Breeder: Any person who produces a litter or breeds a dog.

Breed Rescue: a rescue group that specialized in finding homes for unwanted dogs of a specific breed.

Breed Standard: a description of a breed that describes the physical characteristics as well as temperament to expect in a set breed.

Breeding Particulars: the information about a breeding or litter such as the parents, sex and colour of the puppy and the date of birth.

Brick Shaped: a dog that has a rectangular shape.

Brisket: usually refers to the breastbone or sternum, however, it can also refer to the entire chest and thorax of the dog.

Brood Bitch: used to refer to a female dog that has or will be used for breeding.

Brows: the ridge above the eye.

Brush: when a tail has a heavy amount of hair on it.

Brushing: refers to a gait where the dog's legs brush against each other when he walks.

Butterfly: refers to a nose that has only a small or partial amount of pigmentation on it.

Buttocks: the rump of the dog.

By-products: found in food labels, it refers to any food that is not suitable for human consumption.

Camel Back: a dog that has an arched back.

Canid: refers to any animal in the canidae family such as dogs, wolves and foxes.

Canine: a term for dog.

Canine Teeth: the largest teeth found in the dog's mouth. They are long, curved teeth on either side of the mouth, top and bottom. Also known as eye teeth.

Canter: a run where the dog has three beats.

Cape: refers to longer hair over the shoulders.

Carnivore: an animal that eats only the flesh of other animals.

Carpals: the bones found in the wrist.

Carrier: when a dog carries a disease that it can transmit to other animals without showing any signs of the disease.

Castrate: when the dog's testicles are removed.

Cat Foot: refers to a foot that is round with high-arched toes.

Cheek: the area between the lips and front of ears just under the eyes.

Chest: the area around the ribs.

Chippendale Front: when the dog's forelegs push out at the elbows on the front legs and the feet turn out.

Chiseled: a dog with a head free of bumps and bulges.

Chronic Disease: refers to a disease that will last indefinitely.

Cleft Palate: when the two halves of the mouth do not fuse properly. It is a birth defect.

Clipping: When a dog's back foot hits the front foot when walking.

Cloddy: a dog that is thick and heavy.

Close Mating: used to describe the act of breeding the same female shortly after her previous litter was whelped. The period of time would be less than 4 months and 15 days.

Close Coupled: refers to a short length of body between the last set of ribs and the hind quarters.

Coarse: a dog that is not refined. Also refers to the texture of the coat when it has a hard or rough texture.

Coat: the fur that covers the dog.

Cobby: a dog with a short body.

Colostrum: the clear to yellowish milk produced by a dam during the first 48 hours after her puppies are born.

Concaveation: when a spayed female produces milk.

Condition: the overall look and health of the dog.

Conformation: a term used to describe the physical traits of a breed.

Congenital: a disease or condition that is present at birth. Congenital problems are not necessarily hereditary.

Coupling: refers to the part of the dog's body that is between the ribs and hind quarters.

Cow-hocked: when the dog's hocks turn inward and cause the feet to turn outward.

Crate: Also known as a kennel, the crate is a container that is used for housing dogs.

Crest: the area on the neck that is arched.

Crossbred: when a dog has a dam and sire from different breeds. Also known as a cur.

Croup: the area around the pelvic girdle.

Crown: the top of the head.

Culottes: fur on the upper thighs that is longer and fringe like. Also known as pants, breeches and trousers.

Cur: when a dog has a dam and sire from different breeds. Also known as a crossbreed or mutt.

Cynology: the study of dogs and canines.

Dam: a female dog that is pregnant or has puppies. Also refers to the female parent or mother.

Dander: the skin that is sloughed off of the dog.

Date of Whelping: refers to the date when the puppies are born.

Dealer: an individual who buys puppies from a breeder and then sells the puppies to others. It is recommended that you avoid puppy dealers.

Deep Chest: A dog or dog breed that has a longer chest or rib cage.

Dentition: the number of teeth in an adult dog, which is 42.

Dewclaw: the claw that is found on the inside of the leg above the foot.

Digit: refers to a toe.

Dock: the act of cutting a dog's tail short.

Dog: refers to canines, however, it is also the term used for a male canine.

Domed Skull: a skull that is rounded.

Domesticated: a term used to describe any animal that has been tamed.

Dominance: when a dog has more assertive characteristics. Also describes when a single dog has more influence over other dogs. i.e. he is the dominant dog of the pack.

Double coat: refers to a type of dog coat that has two coats; the soft undercoat that provides warmth and the topcoat that provides protection from the weather and terrain.

Down Hairs: the shortest hairs on a dog, which is usually soft and downy in texture.

Dudley Nose: a nose that has no pigmentation.

Elbow: the area on the posterior of the forearm.

Elbows Out: when a dog's elbows turn away from the body.

Embryo: a term used to describe an undeveloped fetus.

Entire: a dog that has not been altered and its reproductive system is complete. Also called intact.

Estrus: the period of a dog's heat cycle when the female is most receptive to being mated. It precedes ovulation.

Euthanasia: the practice of ending life through medical means.

Even Bite: when the lower and upper incisors have no overlap.

Expression: the features of the head and how they look.

F1: the offspring of a direct crossing of two purebred dogs.

F2: the offspring of one F1 parent and one purebred parent. Could also refer to the offspring of two F1 parents.

F3: the offspring of one F1 parent and one F2 parent. Could also refer to the offspring of two F2 parents.

Fang: the canines.

Feathering: Long hair on the ears, tail, legs or body that has a fringe like appearance.

Feral: a dog that has returned to a wild state.

Fetus: the unborn puppy.

Fever: an indication that there is an illness. The body temperature rises to over 103°F in dogs.

Fiddle Front: when a dog's elbows and feet turn out but the pasterns are close together.

Fillers: found in dog food, it is a chemical or low quality, indigestible food that adds weight to the dog food.

Fixed: a term to describe a dog that has been neutered or spayed.

Flank: the side of a dog's body that is between the hip and last rib.

Flat-Sided: a dog that has flat rib, the desired shape is rounded. Sometimes called slab-sided.

Floating Rib: in dogs, the 13th rib is not attached to the other ribs.

Flying Trot: a run where all four of the dog's feet are off the ground for a second on each half stride.

Foster Mother: a female dog that is nursing puppies that are not her own.

Fresh Extended Semen: this is used in artificial insemination breeding where semen is extracted from a male dog and an extender is placed in the semen to expand the lifespan of the semen.

Frill: refers to longer hair on the chest, also known as the apron.

Front: the part of the dog's body that is in the front. This is the forelegs, shoulder line, chest, head, etc.

Frozen Semen: used in artificial insemination breeding, it is semen that is extracted from the male dog and frozen to be used at a later date.

Furrow: an indentation found in the centre of the skull to the stop at the dog's muzzle.

Gait: the pattern of steps when a dog is in movement.

Gallop: when the dog is running.

Gaskin: the lower thigh on the dog.

Genetically Linked Defects: health problems that are passed from parent to offspring.

Gestation Period: used in breeding, it is the time period between mating and birth.

Get: the offspring of a dog.

Groom: brushing, bathing, trimming and caring for the hygienic needs of the dog's coat.

Guard Hairs: the hairs that are stiffer and longer than the other hairs. Usually protects the dog from the terrain and weather.

Hackles: the hairs found on the back of a dog's neck. It will stand up when the dog is angry or frightened.

Handler: a person who trains, works or shows a dog, also known as an agent.

Haunch Bones: term referring to the hip bones.

Haw: the third eyelid found in dogs.

Head: this is used to describe the front portion of the dog, which includes the muzzle, face, ears and cranium.

Heat: when a dog begins to produce a blood like discharge from her vulva to signal that she is starting her estrus cycle.

Height: height is always measured from the bottom of the foot (ground) to the tallest point on the withers (shoulders).

High in Rear: a dog that has a back end that is higher than its shoulders.

Hock: found in the hind legs, it is the area between the second thigh and metatarsus where there is a collection of bones, also known as the ankle.

Housebreak: training a puppy not to defecate or urinate in the house.

Immunization: when shots are given to a dog to help produce immunity to a specific disease.

Imported Semen: when frozen semen is imported from another country.

In and In: refers to any form of inbreeding in dogs where little consideration is given to the results.

Inbreeding: mating two dogs that are closely related. These include mother to son, daughter to son, sibling to sibling.

Incisors: the upper and lower teeth found at the front of the mouth between the canines. Adult dogs have six upper and six lower.

Incubation Period: the period of time between being infected with a disease and the first symptom appearing.

Interbreeding: breeding dogs that are of different breeds. Also called crossbreeding.

Jacobsens Organ: this is an organ located in the dog's mouth, specifically on the roof, that functions as a sensory organ for taste and smell.

Keel: the rounded area of the chest.

Kennel: Also known as a crate, the kennel is a container that is used for housing dogs. Also used to describe a place that houses and/or breeds dogs. Many breeders use the term loosely to describe a line of dogs, i.e., "Her kennel produces lovely dogs."

Knuckling Over: a condition seen primarily in puppies where the wrist joints flex forward when the dog is standing.

Lactation: the milk that is produced by the mammary glands from a female dog.

Lead: a term used to describe a leash.

Leather: the part of the outer ear that is supported by cartilage.

Line: the pedigree or family of dogs who are related.

Line Breeding: when a dog is bred to another member of its blood line such as grandfather to granddaughter, aunt to nephew, uncle to niece.

Litter: the puppies that are produced during a whelping. It can refer to one puppy or several.

Litter Complement: refers to the number of puppies of each sex in a litter.

Litter Registration: a record with a kennel club of a litter.

Lumbering: refers to a dog with a gait that is awkward.

Mad Dog: refers to a dog that has rabies.

Marking: a behaviour done primarily by males, although it can be seen in females, where a dog will urinate to establish the boundaries of its territory.

Markings: used to describe the patterns found on a dog's coat.

Mask: when there is dark shading on the face.

Mate: when a male dog and female dog are bred.

Maternal Immunity: seen in newborn puppies, it is a resistance to disease that is temporarily passed from mother to pup.

Measure Out: when a dog's height is larger than the breed standard.

Microchip: a small chip that is inserted under the skin. It contains a code that can be scanned and all the owner's information for the dog can be pulled up. Used as identification.

Milk Teeth: the puppy's first teeth, which will fall out to make way for adult teeth during the first year of life.

Molars: the square, posterior teeth that is used for chewing.

Mongrel: when a dog has a dam and sire from different breeds, also known as a crossbreed.

Monorchid: a dog that only has one testicle.

Muzzle: the protruding section of the dog's head which includes the mouth, and nose.

Natural Breed: a breed of dog that developed without human interference. Sometimes called a landrace breed.

Nesting Behaviour: seen in pregnant female dogs or those going through a false pregnancy, it is when the bitch prepares a place to whelp her young.

Neuter: when the dog's testicles are removed.

Nick: refers to a breeding between dogs of two different bloodlines that consistently produces puppies that are desirable according to the breed standard.

Nictitating Membrane: the third eyelid found in dogs.

Odd-Eyed: when one eye is a different colour than the other.

Omnivore: an animal that eats both animal flesh and vegetation.

On-Dog Identification: any form of identification that enables people to identify the dog.

Outcrossing: breeding two dogs that are not related but are still of the same breed.

Overage Dam: an older dam that is older than 7 years old when she is bred.

Overage Sire: an older sire that is older than 12 years old when he is bred.

Overhang: a dog with an overly pronounced brow.

Overshot: when the upper jaw protrudes out and the lower jaw is behind the upper jaw when the mouth is closed.

Ovulate: when the ovary releases a mature ova.

Pants: fur on the upper thighs that is longer and fringe like, also known as breeches, culottes and trousers.

Pack: multiple dogs that live together.

Pedigree: a record of a dog's genealogy.

Pen Breeding: when a breeding occurs due to a male and female dog being penned together. The breeding is not witnessed.

Pile: the dense and soft hair that is the undercoat.

Pinking Up: used to describe a pregnant female dog when her nipples begin to turn pink.

Plucking: the act of pulling out loose hair by hand. Some breeds need to be hand-groomed by plucking.

Purebred: a dog that has parents, grandparents and so on of the same breed.

Quick: the vein that is found in the dog's nail.

Registration Papers: documents from a registry that show proof of breed and whether the dog is purebred.

Scent: the odour that is left in the air or on the ground by an animal.

Scissors Bite: when the lower incisors touch the upper incisors when the dog's mouth is closed.

Season: refers to the period of time when the female dog can be bred.

Secondary Coat: the hairs that are found in the undercoat.

Selective Breeding: when a breeder chooses to breed two dogs together in the hopes of eliminating or achieving a trait.

Septum: the line that is seen between the two nostrils of the dog.

Service Dog: a specially trained dog that works with people who have disabilities.

Show Quality: a dog that is an excellent representation of the breed standard.

Silent Heat: when a female dog goes into heat but shows little or no outward signs that she is in heat.

Single Coat: a dog that does not have an undercoat.

Sire: the male dog, specifically the male parent.

Smooth Coat: a short coat that lays close to the body.

Soundness: a dog that has both mental and physical health functioning properly.

Spay: a procedure where the reproductive organs of a female are removed. This prevents heat and the female from getting pregnant.

Spectacles: when there are dark markings around the eyes.

Spread Hock: refers to legs where the hock turns outward, which makes the feet turn inward, also known as barrel hocks.

Stacking: the way a dog stands when being exhibited in a dog show.

Standing Heat: the period during heat when the female will accept a male and can become pregnant.

Stray Dog: a dog that is lost or homeless.

Teat: the nipple of an animal.

Topcoat: the hairs that are stiffer and longer than the other hairs.

Usually protects the dog from the terrain and weather.

Trousers: fur on the upper thighs that is longer and fringe like, also known as pants, culottes and breeches.

Tuck Up: the waist of the dog where the body is shallower in depth.

Typey: a dog that exhibits the conformation of the breed standard.

Underage Dam: a female dog that is bred before she is 8 months of age.

Underage Sire: a male dog that is bred before he is 7 months of age.

Undershot: when the lower jaw protrudes past the upper jaw when the mouth is closed.

Unsound: refers to a dog that is physically or mentally unable to perform in the way it was intended.

Vaccine: a shot that is given to a dog to help produce immunity to a specific disease.

Variety: when one breed has several subtypes, such as long haired and short haired, but both subtypes can be interbred.

Vent: the anus or anal opening.

Wean: the process of switching a puppy from milk to solid foods.

Weedy: a dog that lacks the musculature that is described in the standard.

Whelp Date: the date when the litter is born.

Whelping: this is the term used to describe a dam giving birth.

Withers: the top of the shoulders of the dog.

Zoonosis: a disease that can be passed from animal to human.

Chapter Fourteen: Resources

Now that you know everything you can about the Tibetan Mastiff, here are some resources that will help make owning your Tibetan Mastiff easier. These are both specific breed resources for the Tibetan Mastiff and general dog resources.

Tibetan Mastiff Resources

The first resources that you should have on hand are those related directly to your Tibetan Mastiff. Some excellent ones to start with are:

American Tibetan Mastiff Association
http://www.tibetanmastiff.org/

Tibetan Mastiff Rescue, Inc.
http://www.tibetanmastiffrescueinc.org/

The Tibetan Mastiff Club of Great Britan
http://www.tmcgb.net/

Tibetan Mastiff Info
http://www.tibetanmastiffinfo.com/

Canada's Guide To Dogs
http://www.canadasguidetodogs.com/tibetanmastiff.htm

Tibetan Mastiff Breeders

It is not always easy to find Tibetan Mastiff breeders. Even the parent clubs for this breed do not currently list any breeders. Here are some breeders with web sites online. We are not necessarily recommending these breeders but you can visit their sites to see their photos and find out if they have litters planned. As always, please investigate any breeder in whom you are interested.

Himalaya Tibetan Mastiffs
www.tibetan-mastiffs.net/foundation.shtml

Sierras Tibetan Mastiffs
www.sierrastibetanmastiffs.com/about.shtml

TIMBERLINE TMs - Timberline Tibetan Mastiffs
timberlinetibetanmastiffs.com/timberline_tibetan_mastiff.html

Drakyi Tibetan Mastiffs
www.tibetanmastiff.com/

Citadel Tibetan Mastiffs
www.tibetanmastiff.net/

Great Lakes Tibetan Mastiffs
www.greattibetanmastiffs.com/

Dawa Tibetan Mastiffs
dawatm.com/

Nyingma Tibetan Mastiffs
www.mytibetanmastiffs.com/

Comancheria Tibetan Mastiffs
www.comancheriatms.com/

AUJUDONTIBETAN MASTIFFS
www.aujudontibetanmastiffs.com/

SnowSpirits Tibetan Mastiffs
www.snowspiritstibetanmastiffs.com/

Kennel Clubs

When it comes to dogs, kennel clubs are an important part of the dog world. The Tibetan Mastiff is a very old breed but it is relatively new to many Western countries. Visit these kennel club web sites to learn more about the Tibetan Mastiff in their countries. Kennel clubs can often refer you to breeders in their countries.

American Kennel Club: http://www.akc.org/
Australian National Kennel Council: http://www.ankc.org.au/
Canadian Kennel Club: http://www.ckc.ca/en
Danish Kennel Club: http://www.dkk.dk/
Estonian Kennel Union: http://kennelliit.ee/en/
FCI: http://www.fci.be/
Finnish Kennel Club: http://www.kennelliitto.fi/
French Kennel Club: http://lifestream.aol.com/
German Kennel Club: http://www.vdh.de/home/
Italian Kennel Club: http://www.cta.it/
Irish Kennel Club: http://www.ikc.ie/
Japan Kennel Club: http://www.jkc.or.jp/
New Zealand Kennel Club: http://www.nzkc.org.nz/
Norwegian Kennel Club: http://www.nkk.no/
Swedish Kennel Club: http://www.skk.se/
Swiss Kennel Club: http://www.skg.ch/cms/home.html
United Kennel Club: http://www.ukcdogs.com/
The Kennel Club: http://www.thekennelclub.org.uk/

Dog Owner Resources

Finally, here are a few dog owner resources that will help you navigate your way through pet ownership. It is important to note that we are not affiliated with any of these sites. Always discuss your dog's health and training issues with trained professionals.

AltVetMed: http://www.altvetmed.org/
American College of Veterinary Nutrition: http://www.acvn.org/
American Dog Trainers Network: http://www.inch.com/~dogs/
Breeder.net: http://www.breeders.net/
Canine Eye Registration Foundation: http://web.vmdb.org/home/CERF.aspx
Canine Health Foundation: http://www.akcchf.org/
DogAware: http://dogaware.com/
Canine Health Information Center: http://www.caninehealthinfo.org/
Dog Owners' Guide: http://www.canismajor.com/
Dog Time: http://dogtime.com/
Dr. Foster and Smith Pet Education: http://www.peteducation.com/
Healthy Pet: http://www.aaha.org/pet_owner/
Medline Plus: http://www.nlm.nih.gov/medlineplus/pethealth.html
Orthopedic Foundation for Animals: http://www.offa.org/
PAW: http://www.paw-rescue.org/
Pet Diets: https://www.petdiets.com/
Pet Loss: http://www.petloss.com/
Pet-Loss Support: http://www.pet-loss.net/
PetMD: http://www.petmd.com/
Pet Pharmacy: http://www.veterinarypartner.com
Petstyle: http://www.petstyle.com/
Rainbow Bridge Pet Loss: https://rainbowsbridge.com/
Terrific Pets: http://www.terrificpets.com/

VetInfo: http://www.vetinfo.com/
Vetmedicine: http://vetmedicine.about.com/
Vetquest: http://www.vetquest.com/
Whole Pet: http://www.wholepetvet.com/

Photo Credits

The photos within this book have kindly been donated by:

www.ingramcontent.com/pod-product-compliance
Lightning Source LLC
Chambersburg PA
CBHW030436010526
44118CB00011B/665